BROKEN SILENCE

A TRUE STORY OF A SIXTEEN YEAR OLD'S CAPTIVITY IN EVIN...IRAN'S MOST FEARED PRISON!

KATHY A. TAHERI

IUNIVERSE, INC.
BLOOMINGTON

Broken Silence
A true story of a sixteen year old's captivity
in Evin...Iran's most feared prison!

iUniverse books may be ordered through booksellers or by contacting:

iUniverse
1663 Liberty Drive
Bloomington, IN 47403
www.iuniverse.com
1-800-Authors (1-800-288-4677)

ISBN: 978-1-4502-8777-7 (sc)
ISBN: 978-1-4502-8776-0 (dj)
ISBN: 978-1-4502-8775-3 (ebk)

Library of Congress Control Number: 2011900579

Printed in the United States of America

iUniverse rev. date: 1/20/2011

This book is dedicated to the amazing people all over the world who have been held captive, tortured or died in prisons for standing up for their beliefs and speaking for those who could not speak for themselves.

*There is no greater agony
than
bearing an untold story
inside you…*

Maya Angelou

CONTENTS

ACKNOWLEDGMENT

To start, I would like to thank God for giving me the courage and strength to write this book. I always felt that an extraordinary presence gently held me through this journey. It carried me through the hills and valleys of those painful emotions so this story could manifest at the right place and the right time. What I call God, some people call Universal Intelligence; but it really is not important what we call it. What matters is that I was able to feel its powerful presence during the toughest times of my life though it seemed that I was all alone.

A special thanks goes out to my counselor, coach, editor, mentor and guide, Louise Bailey, without whom I might never have dared to put myself, my family and my life out there in front of millions of people. Louise, thank you for believing in me when I did not believe in myself; for putting up with me when I was not patient with myself; and for going above and beyond the call of duty to keep me on my path and care for me as much as you did. I truly appreciate you in my life and I could not have done this without you.

Also I would like to extend my heartfelt gratitude to a great scholar, artist and writer, Michael Hillsey, who is my editor, my guide and my best friend for supporting me on my path every step of the way. As my editor, you have granted me the wish to write with total freedom and do this using my own voice. And as my best friend and my guide, you have always been an inspiration for me and an amazing source of peace and serenity. Michael, you light up my life and make my world a better place without a doubt.

I would also like to thank my best friend, my business coach and my mentor, Cindy Hillsey, who shared laughter and tears with me throughout this project. To you Cindy, I want to say: I love and appreciate you more than it is possible to express with words here; you have been a source of motivation and drive for me and you have made a huge difference in my life. I am so thankful to have you in my life.

Last but not least I would like to thank my teacher, and mentor, Joe Gaskovski who has taught me to focus on my strengths and to take a forward movement toward my goals in the face of fear and uncertainty. Joe, you have certainly been a positive influence in my life and I thank you for being there for me always.

Throughout the years, I have been blessed with amazing friends who have touched my heart and soul in so many ways. Though I won't be able to name all of those special people here, I would like to name the two extraordinary people who made a tremendous difference in my life. Zahra and Pari were there for me through the most painful times of my life and I could not imagine my life without them. I want to take this opportunity to extend my deepest love, gratitude and appreciation to those two angels and to each and every one of my friends. I blossomed because they believed in me and loved me unconditionally. They were always there to pick up the pieces each time I fell apart. To all of my incredible friends, my earth angels, I would like to say this: You honor me and I love you with all my heart!

Mostly, however, I want to thank my amazing children, Siavash and Afsheen who have been true joy and blessings in my life and absolutely the best thing that could ever happen to me. Those of us who are parents know that parenthood has its challenges to say the least. As parents we are not always patient and understanding with our children; but one truth remains unshakable and that is our unconditional LOVE towards our children. I want to say to my two wonderful sons, that I have always loved you with all my heart. With every fiber of my being, I longed to see you two happy and healthy throughout your lives. My life has been worthy of living because of the both of you. I am so very proud of you. I hope you find it in your hearts to forgive me for what I was and was not supposed to say; what I was and was not supposed to do and for what I was and was not supposed to be as a mother. I don't feel that I have been able to give you everything you deserved except my undying love and appreciation. If I had a chance to start all over again and to choose my children, I would still choose the two of you; but this time I would work harder to become a more patient and understanding mother so as to deserve such miraculous treasures in my life. No matter where I am and what I am doing, you are both with me; in my heart and my mind and I cherish every moment that we have spent together as a family. I love you both more than life itself.

I would also like to thank my parents and my brothers and sisters who have always made me feel loved and cared for. Though we had different outlooks of life and might not have seen eye to eye in many cases, I always knew they would be there for me if and when I needed them. Thank you all for your endless love, patience and support.

PREFACE

After almost three decades I finally found the courage to tell my story. Many times I was tempted to give up on this book all together. I knew writing my story would mean reliving the most painful times of my life; and I was not sure if I could ever be ready for that. I was tempted to leave the past in the past, so to speak, and not to bring up the unpleasant memories I had tried so hard to forget for decades. Ironically, my life up to this point was a proof that one cannot leave the past in the past unless they have dealt with it properly. While this inner struggle was going on, a loud and powerful voice inside me kept this desire alive. It was as though I could not move on with my life and heal my wounds unless I acted upon this desire. As I went on ignoring my gut feeling in this regard, I felt cowardly and shameful. I did not realize that perhaps the time was not right for me to undertake such strenuous task.

As days turned into weeks, weeks into months, and months into years, I finally felt that the time was right to tell my story. It was then when I realized that I had actually picked the perfect time to share my story with the world. I intuitively knew that the purpose of this book had to unfold before me so I could start writing. I sensed that I could not turn this desire into reality when fear was still running my life. And when I was still imprisoned in my self-made prison of shame, anger, blame, resentment, judgement, guilt and despair. All those years, I was nowhere near the space I needed to be to undertake such a worthy and complex project. I lived in constant fear that if I ever got experienced true happiness that would all be taken away from me. It felt safer just to stay unhappy; at least such pain and misery was familiar to me.

I had no self-love, self-esteem, or self-respect. The scars I carried inside of me were so big that I was unable to function properly. I felt like a person whose spirit had left her body long ago, and indeed that was true. Many times when I was alone, I spoke with God and asked why my life was spared in prison. I wondered if I had done something wrong, perhaps in my past life, and I was reborn to be punished for it. I wondered why everything and everyone that meant something to me was taken away from me so violently.

I often cried, thinking that God must be asleep because he was not talking to me. It never occurred to me that perhaps I have stopped listening; or perhaps my heart was not open to receive him. It never occurred to me then that this could be part of a bigger plan the universe had in store for me. Could it be that I appeared in this world, was born in Iran, and into my family to fulfill a much greater purpose than I could grasp at the time?

It took couple of decades of pain and agony before I was able to change my outlook of life and see the big picture. Thereafter, I was able to see clearly my responsibility to speak up, break my silence, and share my sorrowful experience with the world. I heard somewhere that the best way to predict the future is to create it. That phrase resonated with me for I truly believe that as I changed my outlook of life and stopped being a victim, I started to take an active part in creating my own destiny. My new outlook provided me with the conviction I needed to see this project through. I finally understood that what made me a victim was not so much the circumstances of my life, but how I responded to them. With this new discovery, I became more determined to share my story. I could not stand the thought of another human being giving up on their dreams. I felt that if sharing my experience can help even one person to break free of their victim mentality, then the emotional roller coaster ride of this project will have been worth it.

And here is how my story began. It all started at the age of 16 when four armed government agents came to pay me a visit at my mom's hospital bed. I was arrested that night and taken away from my mother and my family and unjustly held captive in Iran's most feared prison,

Evin. This was the beginning of my agonizing experience. Life as I once knew it changed forever.

As a political prisoner, my crime was reading books that the Iranian government deemed banned and supporting opposition parties that openly criticized our regime for violating basic human rights. Even as a teenager, the following comments made perfect sense to me: people should be free to choose their own religion; they should be free to examine different schools of thought by reading books or newspapers of their choice; they should be able to express their opinion on issues that directly impact the quality of their lives without fear of retribution; that women should not lose their children if they decide to divorce their husbands; and they should not have to tolerate staying in abusive relationships because our culture condemned divorce. I believed that regardless of our race, gender, belief, status, and financial power, we all had the right to live without fear and terror. I believed that we all had the right to live with dignity and respect.

This true story is about a young girl with big dreams and even bigger heart. A girl who loved school and had an unquenchable thirst to learn. A girl who freely expressed her thoughts and beliefs; and a girl who wanted to speak for those who could not speak for themselves. As you turn the pages of this book, you will hear a bit about my family history and how I grew up. I will then help you see how my life unfolded at the age of 13, after Iran's revolution, all the way to my imprisonment, my first job, my marriage, my first born, leaving my country and my life in Canada.

Last but not least, I would like to apologize to my family if they feel offended to some degree by reading this story. I have always loved and respected my family and I have no doubt that they all love me too. However, I feel that disclosing information about my family might seem like a distasteful act on my part. If this is the case, while I appreciate, understand, and respect their point of view on this matter, I want to emphasize that the information disclosed here about my family, has emanated solely from my unique perspective of our family dynamic and my place in it. I am sure each one of us perceives our environment and our family differently; the story of my childhood is only my version of the truth about all of us as a family. When I decided to write this book, I was not planning to write about my family background as I was concerned about how my family would receive that. However, it felt right to provide my readers with little bit of background about my life throughout my childhood and the type of family I grew in so as to assist them in better understanding why my life unfolded the way it did. This book is about my life experience as a child and as an adult and as such I have only depicted information about our family that directly ties into my story.

The opening chapter of this book is about my mom, who passed away many years ago, since she is the main character in my story. She has always lived in my heart and my mind and I always felt that she was watching over me. She held me under her wings through the most challenging experiences of my life and gave me the strength to get up each time I fell. Though I wish she was here with me physically, I know in my heart that she has always been part of my life. Her untimely death shattered our family and though we suffered so much when we lost her, her love and strength kept us alive and well. I don't believe I quite understood or appreciated her when she was with us, but I certainly believe that I got to know her intimately when she left this world. All I am and all I have is because of my mom. She has lived in my heart and will go on living inside me forever.

My mom is a never-ending song in my heart of comfort, happiness, and being. I may sometimes forget the words but I always remember the tune. (Graycie Harmon)

++ +++++++++

It was well past midnight as we still tossed and turned trying, unsuccessfully, to fall asleep. Deep in a world of our own, we were brought back to consciousness by agonizing hollers from far away. A man was pleading for mercy, begging his assailers to stop beating him. His horrific screams echoed through the hallways. We cringed and trembled as his dreadful cries for help intensified. Panic and anxiety took our breath away.

A sudden shiver took over my body. My heart was pounding as every fiber of my body ached. It was as though I was the one being beaten. "Was I going out of my mind, imagining all this, or was this all real?", I thought to myself. Dry-mouth and covered in cold sweat, I crawled in and reached for my friends' hands. They too, were shaking. None of us had experienced anything like this before. Our muffled cries soon turned into choked whispers as we prayed for the man. We covered our ears, trying helplessly not to be involved in such an appalling encounter.

The heart wrenching screams went on for about ten minutes before they came to a sudden stop. Immobilized by fear, we let out our breath. A deafening silence had pinned us to the floor. Perhaps the man had lost consciousness. The beating had stopped, yet our apprehension had deepened. We now feared he might be dead!

Distraught, we held hands looking for comfort. We were all ears hoping to hear if he was still alive. Each moment felt like an eternity. We had almost lost hope when we suddenly heard a weak cry coming from far away. We sat motionless waiting to hear him again. We could hear a pin drop in our cell. A few endless minutes passed before we could hear a frail moaning. The man's cries spoke of his excruciating pain. Shortly after, we heard him dragged through the hallways. Perhaps he was not of much use to them now. As his limp body passed down the gloomy hallways, we said our goodbyes tearfully. We felt we had known him for a long time. We never knew who he was or what he looked like. And we never found out what happened to him.

The oppressive silence took Ward 209 under its wings again. Though the commotion had ended, none of us were able to get much sleep. We laid down quietly staring at the ceiling with our eyes wide open, wondering if we could bear such vicious torture. We dreaded our own fate as we cried ourselves to sleep.

We felt invisible. Our survival was threatened. We had been stripped off our dignity, slowly but surely. It was unfathomable to witness such brutality at the hands of those who, in the name of God, acted like trained killers. Fear nibbled us. A profound sadness had fallen upon us. My heart was breaking into pieces. My body trembled. My hands were shaking violently. There was no light at the end of this tunnel. Exhausted, anguished and hopeless, I looked for God everywhere...

CHAPTER 1 –
MY MOM:

"No painter's brush, nor poet's pen
in justice to her fame
has ever reached half high enough
to write a mother's name."
(Unknown Author)

****

My mom was born into a large family. Out of six children she was the third. She was very different from her brother and four sisters in many ways. In addition to her stunning outer beauty, she had a radiant personality and a heart as big as the sky. No one in her family loved books, school or learning as much as she did, and none of her siblings were as free spirited and outspoken as she was. She was a passionate woman who truly believed in serving others and helping disadvantaged people anyway she could. A profession she chose well suited her personality. She became a nurse and a midwife. She gladly volunteered to take on pregnant women from poor families as patients knowing that they could not afford to pay for her services. And if that family was extremely poor, she would help them out in anyway possible without offending the families. To cover babies basic needs, she would purchase clothing, formulas and other necessary items and would take it to them as a gift. And if new moms just had their first babies, she would also take time, free of charge, to educate them on how to take best care of their babies and themselves after the delivery.

She inspired others by just being herself and sharing her love with others. At home she was the special child adored by everyone in her family. My mom was always eager to learn new things and while for some of those skills she had taken classes, mostly she would learn things by just watching others. She was a quick learner and extremely intelligent woman. She learned sewing, knitting, cooking, baking and hair styling after she graduated from university and later on when she was working full time. Even as a mother of five and a wife, she never gave up on her schooling. She continued with her studies until she obtained her masters degree in nursing.

My grandfather loved my mother very much but he had much difficulty keeping her in line. He was an old fashioned, religious man who was totally against women's education. He especially had a problem with my mom going off to school. She was a very pretty woman and my grandfather thought that she would be corrupted. He associated going to university with becoming out of control and sinful. Consequently, he opposed her every step of the way.

My mother used to tell us that she snuck her books into a small bathroom outside in the backyard and read under the dim light in the cold so that her father did not get on her case. At times, she waited for her father to fall sleep so she could get started on her assignments and school activities. With the help of people who had some influence on her dad, she finally was given permission, very hesitantly, to go to University where she later graduated with a degree in nursing.

My mom used to say, that those days in the university were the best days of her life. But her bachelor degree in nursing was not enough for her. My mom wanted to continue her education in Europe as she dreamed of obtaining her PHD or perhaps studying to become a medical doctor. One of many things I admired about my mom was her passion for learning and education.

My grandfather had different plans for my mom. He wanted to choose a man so she could get married and have children as soon as possible. He did not want to hear any nonsense about further education. My mom knew that this time she was not going to win. She hoped that at least her father would consider her wishes and let her have a say in who she would marry. Given that she was very pretty, my mom had quite a few admirers at the hospital where she worked; among those she was interested in were a couple of doctors who were willing to go to her dad and ask him for her hand in marriage. But my grandfather was adamant that he pick the one that he thought was best for her. "Doctors are not good enough for marriage", he would say; "they look at naked bodies all day long and I will not hear any more nonsense about this".

So he chose my dad! My grandfather liked my dad a lot and they had a great relationship as son-in-law and father-in-law. My father had come from a well known, wealthy and respected family and he was gainfully employed as an officer in the army. My father was respectful of elders and had tremendous respect for who my grandfather was. My grandfather found my father a genuine and loving man deserving of marring his daughter. Possessing such favourable qualities opened up the possibility for my father to marry my mother. In addition, my father had a great sense of humour, loved children and was easy going.

As difficult as it might be to fathom such circumstances, in those days, parents had full authority in finding husbands or wives for their children. Arranged marriages were very common yet those who were forced to live by their parents rules were rarely happy. The situation was much worse for women since they were not considered as equals to men. As a result, they absolutely had no say in who they would want to marry or even if they wanted to get married. My mom did not get to see my father before the day she married him!

My mom believed that her father thought he knew what was best for her. She was convinced that my grandfather behaved in such a way out of love and concern for her; nevertheless, that did not make things any easier for my mom. Saying good bye to one's dreams is never easy; but my mom had to accept her fate. With a heavy heart she finally became a bride. My mom's apprehension was obvious even in her wedding photo. My mom looked absolutely stunning on her wedding day. Her wedding dress was gorgeous; her full, shiny black hair was styled in a simple yet elegant manner, and her make up, while very light, certainly added to her natural beauty. She looked like a movie star. But underneath all that glamour, it was easy to see her grief by looking at her big, beautiful brown eyes. Her eyes told the story of a broken heart and shattered dreams.

My father on the other hand, was very happy to know that he could finally have my mom. He had seen a picture of my mom and knew that he was marrying a pretty woman. Truly, my mom was the whole package; she had brains, beauty and a heart bigger than the entire universe. While my father had great qualities as well, he was just too different from my mom and certainly not the person that my mom would have picked if she was free to choose her own partner.

As soon as my parents got married, my father asked my mom to quit her job. While she absolutely loved her job, she had to listen to her husband. My father was very insecure. He believed that my mom was just too pretty and that he might lose her to some other men at work.

It took my mom almost eight years and four children before she was allowed to return to her career; and that was after I was born. I believe by then my father had built enough trust to allow his wife to go back to work. Perhaps he thought after so many years of marriage and four children, no one could come between them so he agreed that my mom pick up where she left off and return to work.

I had heard this story from my mom before so when she was mad at me for being mischievous, I could easily get off the hook. All I had to do to turn things around was to remind my mom that the happiest occasions in her life happened after I was born. Perhaps if it was not for me, she would not have gone back to work and that had to count for something! That comment would make my mom laugh and soon she would forgive and forget my naughty behaviour.

I resemble my mom in so many ways. Some even say that I physically look like her more than her other children, but I believe I am more similar to her in spirit. Just like my mom, I had passion for life; I was passionate about school and learning; I had a vision of how my life should turn out; and last but not least, I was stubborn, determined and very much idealistic. Perhaps that was the reason my mom and I rarely saw eye to eye. Since I resembled her so much, in so many ways, she must have feared that eventually I might share the same fate.

Chapter 2 -
My Family History:

"In each family a story is playing itself out, and each family's story embodies its hope and despair." (Auguste Napier)

****

I was born and raised in Tehran, Iran. I was born into a middle class family that consisted of my mom, dad, two older sisters and an older brother. My mom was a nurse, and a midwife, and my dad was a colonel in the army. At any given time, we also had one or two live-in housekeepers to help my parents take care of the house and children. My parents lead a busy life as both of them worked full time. We always had a full house as my parents loved guests. And sometimes a few of our relatives would stay with us two or three months at a time so I would say we were a large family. While I resembled my mom so much, I had taken after my dad in some ways too. Like my dad, I was a pet lover, and I loved having guests around all the time so living in such busy household was truly enjoyable for me. We had some relatives who lived in a different city but they had come to live with us for a couple of years while they attended school in Tehran. My parents truly needed help with house work, children, extended family and handling that many guests so the housekeepers were absolute necessity for them on those days.

In Iran at that time, it was mandatory for everyone, both men and women who reached the age of 18, to serve in the army or be assigned to community work such as teaching for two years before they were eligible to enter the workforce. If anyone wanted to get into the university after finishing high school, they were able to on the condition that they would be serving after they finished university. But for those who did not want to enter the university right away, there was no choice but to commit to those two years before getting a job. Of course, like many other things in life, money could be a solution to such issues most of the time. If people could find the right connection to bribe, they could get off the two year mandatory service quite easily. Depending on gender and the amount of education, people would get assigned to different kinds of community services. I remember most girls who had high school diplomas would end up teaching in schools in really small towns or villages where most teachers were not willing to work. Common practice was to assign women to community work and assign men to serve in the army. Many young men, especially boys from farms or villages, who only had an elementary school education, were eager to complete their two year service so they could go back and take charge of their fathers' farms. Those types of soldiers were given an option to serve at the army base either to volunteer two years to work as housekeepers, butlers or drivers at one of the high ranking officers' homes. This would count as the time served for them and they could move on with their lives after they completed their assignment. As surprising as it might sound, quite a few of those young men were interested in living at the house, of one of the officers, instead of staying at the army base.

Getting a free housekeeper, a driver, or a butler for two years was one of the benefits that high ranking army officers would enjoy. Given that we had a full house with working parents, my dad took advantage of that benefit and we always had live-in housekeepers. Every two years we would get new people to help my parents with cleaning, cooking, taking the children to and from school and looking after the pets. Since my father was a pet lover, we had quite a few pets at home that needed special care, and cleaning after them appeared to be a full time job. We had a dog, a cat, a chicken, a rooster, a duck, a turkey, several small cute yellow chicks and couple of beautiful canaries. Our house was not too big but we had a nice backyard so somehow we were able to house all those animals, our housekeepers and ourselves comfortably.

As mentioned before, most often, we had an out of town visitor, one of our extended family, staying with us for few months at the time; and I have fond memories of the time they stayed with us. I was very affectionate and always got a lot of attention from our immediate family. But at times I was able to annoy a few people in our family and my dad's aunt was one of them. I remember when I was about six or seven years old and she was visiting us. Obviously at that age, I had no concept of what getting old could mean to some people. I was very inquisitive and sometimes fascinated by things that most children my age did not care for much. I remember chasing my father's aunt around to find out how old she was; I practically chased her from one room to another. She resented my questions and would tell me to run along and mind my own business. But I just couldn't give up. For some strange reason, I was fascinated to find the correct answer and would not leave it alone. The more she resisted me, the more interested I became to chase her around. Finally, I got tired of chasing her and went straight to my dad to find out if he knew how old his aunt was. Luckily for me, he knew and he did not mind sharing that information with me. It felt so wonderful to finally get the answer to my question, as though I had won the game now. Every chance I got I told my aunt how old she was! That made my aunt really mad but she knew that I was only being a nosy and spoiled six year old who loved having her around. The story I just shared is one of many wonderful stories of my childhood. When I recall those days, regardless of sad occasions in our life, I feel that I had a happy childhood.

My parents were easy going but there were certain rules that we all had to follow. One of those was to treat our housekeepers with utmost respect, much like members of our family. At meal time, my mom would prepare a big tray of food and ask one of us to deliver it to housekeepers' rooms before we could start eating ourselves. We would be punished if we talked down to our housekeepers or if we attempted to disturb them after certain hours in a day. They were entitled to a day off during the week and they had summer and New Year holidays too. They would normally go back to visit their families but if they chose to stay home, we could not ask them to do anything for us as they were being treated like one of us . Our housekeepers had a private room and my parents always made sure they had pocket money as well. I remember my younger siblings and I used to love playing with our housekeepers, who were also very young and playful. When our parents were not around we could be as naughty as we wanted to be. They would not report us to our parents and in return, we never reported them to our parents either. Sometimes they would leave the house to go grocery shopping and would end up in a movie theatre instead. When my father asked them what they were doing for the past couple of hours they would reply that they could not find what they were looking for at the grocery place close by so they had to travel far to get the groceries from another place. And when we were alone with them they would tell us that they had gone and seen a movie and would share how the movie was and what it was about.

In summer, we would play soccer or volleyball and if our parents were not home, we would chase them around the backyard to throw some water at them or push them in a small water fountain in our backyard. Winter was another favourite time of the year for us. We always made snowmen together and threw snow balls at each other. One time when our neighbour's children and we were playing, our housekeepers came to help us attack them with the snow balls. We ended up winning but in the process we broke another neighbour's window with the snow ball. We promised each other not to tell our parents. At times when we bugged them, they would threaten to tell our parents; and we would threaten them back by repeating the name of the movie they had just seen so to get them to see that we were even! It was as if we were living with our cousins; so life was one big happy playground for us.

I kept my position as the youngest sibling in the family for four years before my mom gave birth to a beautiful baby boy. He truly brought so much love and happiness into our lives as he was such a calm, peaceful and affectionate baby. I never recall feeling jealous toward him. He was my new playmate and I loved spending time with him. Several years passed by and I thought our family would not grow larger; but one day my mom announced that she was pregnant. She was very apprehensive about her pregnancy since she had five older children, 17, 16, 13, 11 and 7, and she did not envision having the sixth child in her early forties. At 42, she did not think she could start all over again with another baby. She loved us all very much but she also loved her career and she was not sure if, with her plate already full, she would have the time and energy to pay enough attention to a new baby. My father on the other hand, was very much excited at the prospect of having his sixth child. He was absolutely crazy about children and made a promise to my mom that he would take an active part in caring for the new baby just like he had done with the other children. A promise well kept while my mom was alive.

Nine months later, my mom gave birth to a beautiful healthy baby girl. Her presence lit up our lives since much like my younger brother, she was sweet, loving, warm and very calm. I remember how wonderfully she blended into our family and how close she was with me. It was fun to watch my baby sister chase our pets and play with them. When she started talking, perhaps around the age of two, she was advising and counselling our cat and our chicken, who were constantly at each other's throats. She was asking them to stop fighting and just get along! Even at that young age, she was matured beyond her age. And she was truly the best thing that happened to our family.

Even though I was the fourth child, I still received a lot of attention from my family as I was a happy child: warm, affectionate and very much adaptable in so many ways. My unique gift was my genuine smile and warm heart. I was well liked and cared for by everyone; and I thrived in knowing that I was welcome among family, friends and neighbours. There was another side to me that made my childhood more interesting and perhaps more challenging to my parents. While I was quiet, content, happy and cooperative, I could also be very naughty, stupidly careless, and very much stubborn. I remember when I was in Kindergarten my father took me with him to a city where he was assigned to work for a year (Shiraz). My aunt and her mom lived in that city and since I was close with them, I had agreed to go with my dad and stay with them for few months at least if not for the full year. My father did not know how well I would do without my mom so he was ready to take me back to Tehran if and when I felt home sick. I loved travelling with my father and having his attention all to myself. My aunt absolutely adored me so when she was not in university she would take me everywhere with her. Her friends were also in charge of entertaining me so I would not cry for my mom. When we got together with her friends, they always danced for me and kept me amused at all times. Despite missing my mom and my siblings, I stayed with my dad during his trip and only visited my mom and the rest of my family during my father's time off.

The kindergarten I was enrolled at was not too close so my father ensured that school bus picked me up and dropped me off every day. One day, I came back from school and knocked on the door. No one opened the door but since the entrance door was full length glass, I could see someone walking there. I knocked on the door again and still no response. I knew my aunt and my dad were not home at that time but my great aunt, the same aunt I chased around to find out how old she was, was home. Apparently she was sweeping the floors and she wanted to pick up the garbage before she let me in. I waited for a few minutes and then kicked the door, broke the glass enough to be able to put my hands in and open the door knob. I got in and looked at my great aunt who was looking back at my with her eyes wide open. I asked why she was not opening the door. She was upset with me so all she said was that she would tell my father and my aunt, her daughter, what I had done as soon as they got home. Feeling no remorse for what I had done, I told her that I was the one who would be telling on her about all this. I explained that when I tell them you would not open the door for me, they would understand that I had no choice but to break in. She had a hard time keeping a straight face and not to laugh at my logic. Later on when my father and aunt arrived, I rushed to tell them what had happened acting so innocently that they could not be upset with me. They both laughed and told my great aunt that next time she should open the door immediately; yet they made me promise not to break the glass door again even if my great aunt did not come to door too quickly.

This was not the only naughty story I recall of my childhood. The worst is yet to come!

I must have been nine years old at the time. We had about six or seven neighbours whose houses were on the same street as ours. My siblings and I were best friends with the neighbours' kids. We went to school together; we played together after school, and we stayed at each others' houses from time to time. One summer day as we were on the street playing, we heard horrific screams for help. We rushed to where the noise was coming from and found our best friend's mom in the kitchen screaming for help. A gas leak had caused a fire in the kitchen and she could not find her way out. Pretty soon, fire fighters arrived, put down the fire and rushed her to a hospital near by. Unlike what we thought, her injuries were too severe and despite all that doctors did for her, she died. My brother and I tried to spend more time with our friends to help distract them as much as possible. During such difficult time, I behaved more like an adult trying to comfort our friends as much as possible. A few months passed and things slowly went back to normal. I was slowly missing my playful side where I looked at the world as one big happy playground! It was time for something interesting again. So one night, it must have been just before my bedtime around 9 pm or so, I went to our storage room where we kept extra sheets, pillows and comforters for guests. I picked up a white sheet, put it on my head and left the house without anyone seeing me. I was on the street standing under the kitchen window of the young mother who had passed away only a few months ago. I was playing ghost that night! Changing my voice, I called on our friends: "Hello…it is me, the ghost of your mother"; Come to me my children"; "I have come to take you with me"; "I have heard you have been pretty naughty lately"; "Come… it is time now…let's go". I kept making strange ghostly noises calling for our friends but thankfully no one heard me. Soon however, I felt that the young mother's ghost might come down and take me; so while calling out for my mom, I took the sheet off and ran toward our house. I cringe as I write this story knowing how awfully naughty I was!

Not only I was playful with others, I was bold and carefree when I played on my own. One time I almost fell off our neighbours' flat roof (the house was three stories tall) while jumping from one roof to another. Growing up with two brothers, my playmates were mostly boys. I believed I could do all that the boys could do and perhaps more. Yet I never dressed properly for such ventures. That day when I jumped, I had a long skirt on and it got caught on the railings around the flat roof. It was a miracle that I was able to hold on to the railings and not fall or perhaps I would not be here today to write about it today!

It was as though two people lived inside me and both were free to come out anytime. On one hand I was nurturing, sensitive, confident

11

and responsible; that was my adult side perhaps. And on the other hand, I was naïve, sheltered, overly confident, mischievous, and a trouble maker; that was my playful child side. The adult part of me took life too seriously and felt a profound sadness inside. Yet the child part of me behaved as though life was just an interesting game; she was bold, free spirited and full of zest for life.

I must have been six or seven years old when I started asking questions about the purpose of life and God, whom I had heard was responsible for the creation of the universe. Many times I went to bed with such thoughts dreaming about the time that our universe had not yet come to existence. I still remember those dreams almost four decades later. In almost all of those dreams I saw our neighbourhood without homes, stores, cars, people, birds or anything alive. I was mystified and puzzled. I wanted to know of things that I could not comprehend with my mind yet I could feel them inside me. I felt somehow different from others, but I was too young to know why. My curiosity and fascination with such matters kept me feeling overwhelmed since I did not know who could help answer my questions. I felt I was being pushed toward a certain direction that seemed scary and lonesome. That was the reason that most times, while being surrounded by people who loved me, I felt completely alone.

As I grew older, little by little, I felt more comfortable with myself and was less concerned of how others perceived me. I took pride in befriending the least fortunate kids, academically, financially and those who had come from low social standings in school or in my neighbourhood. I was most content when I could help those kids in some small ways; and sad when I knew there was nothing I could do for them. In school, I was always busy tutoring kids who needed extra help with their studies. In our neighbourhood, I had very many friends. If kids had a falling out with their parents, siblings or friends, I was always there to offer my support. Sometimes all they wanted was for someone to listen to them; and sometimes they needed a shoulder to cry on. My teachers were fond of me too, not only because I was an excellent student, but also because I was helping other students as well. I clearly remember one of my teachers in grade 3 whom I became very close with.

When my siblings and I were still very young, my dad's work often took him away from Tehran, where we all lived, and into different cities in Iran. Sometimes the duration of his temporary work assignments were not too long, but sometimes he had to leave Tehran for a year or two. For shorter assignments in cities that were not too far from Tehran, he did not take his family with him. Instead he would visit us every weekend; and we would visit him during our summer or spring break. There were times, however, that he was assigned work in a city that was far from Tehran and the duration of assignment was anywhere between 12 to 24 months or more. On those occasions he would relocate all of us temporarily to where he had been transferred to. When I was about to start grade 3, my father announced that he had received an assignment in Mashhad, a city which was located 850 KM East of Tehran, for a year and he was taking all of us with him. I remember feeling sad when I heard the news. I knew I would miss my friends, my school, and my cousins whom I was very close with. However, since I knew this was only a temporary move I was not too upset over the whole thing.

The day finally arrived when we packed our stuff and moved to Mashhad. My father rented a house in a nice neighbourhood and we quickly got situated and registered in school. For the most part, my parents did not worry about my siblings and I doing well in school. However, one of my older sisters was not too much into school. My parents were concerned that she was behind in her studies. They tried hard to get her to focus more on school work but nothing seemed to work. My sister was very smart yet she did not enjoy school as much as rest of us did. My parents' frustration escalated to the point that one night, as I was getting ready for bed, I overheard their conversation regarding this issue. My father said that if my sister did not focus on school soon, he was thinking of leaving her behind when it was time for us to leave for Tehran. Perhaps he thought such threats might get my sister to think twice about her actions. I took his words seriously and cried myself to sleep that night. I prayed that my sister would not get separated from the rest of our family. I wanted my family to be whole and complete and that meant having my older sister with us. The next day I got up earlier than usual, dressed up and left for school; at least that was what my parents thought. I had other plans. I had decided to talk to my teacher before the school started that morning. Though

I had known this teacher for less than a year, I felt very comfortable with her. It was as though I had known her for years. She was young, friendly and caring and that was why all of her students liked her a lot. She would always make herself available if any of her students needed help in any area. I knew where she lived since on few occasions after school, we walked together to get home. Her house was just on my way to school so I knew I could quickly get to school after meeting with her. I knocked on the door and she let me in. I could see that she had just woken up as she was still in her nightgown. She saw how upset I was so she quickly asked if everything was okay. When I told her the entire story, she paused for a minute and then asked if I thought the threat was serious. I said that I thought it could be serious. Then she asked how she could be of any assistance and I said that if she could meet with my father, perhaps she could get him to change his mind. She promised that if my father planned to act on his threat, that she would get involved and ask that he reconsider. I immediately felt better; apologized for the inconvenience I had caused and happily went to school. My father never brought up such topics and my teacher did not have to meet with him after all. Obviously he had been venting that night not knowing that I had overheard his conversation. I did not speak of that incident to my friends, my parents or my siblings and my teacher promised to keep it in confidence as well. From that point onward, my teacher and I became closer. She admired my genuine concern for my family; and I appreciated her for empathizing and being there for me when I needed it.

Altogether, I was happy with my life and how it was unfolding; yet, I felt a deep sorrow inside me at the same time. At such a young age, I could sense people's spoken and unspoken sadness when I looked them in the eyes. I got to know people who barely had enough to eat and some who went to bed hungry. I sensed injustices and discriminations based on age, gender, belief or social and financial standings. I was preoccupied by such thoughts and feelings but did not know how to respond all that. I was not sure if I could express my concerns and share my sadness without being looked at as weird. And since I did not feel heard or understood when I talked about such things, I chose to keep silent and bury most of what I felt deep inside me.

Gradually I noticed my parents concern for me. They seemed frustrated not knowing how to get me out of my head so to speak. While I sensed they admired my free spiritedness and big heart, I am sure at times they wished I behaved more like other children my age. By the same token, in so many ways, I was a well-behaved child. I was the quiet one who rarely got into fights with her siblings, friends or classmates. I did not ask for much and did not need supervision to keep up with my school work. If I was asked to do something around the house, I did it with willingness and to the best of my ability. Nevertheless, I always spoke my mind and my parents were afraid that someday I might get me in trouble for that.

I remember when I was 13, without my parents' permission and unannounced, I brought home about ten university students who were Mujahedeen's supporters. They had been staying at a campus next to our building but had been attacked, badly beaten and kicked out of campus by government agents. It was cold and they had nowhere to go and not much money to spend on food. They were in Tehran to finish their studies but most of their families lived in different cities far from Tehran. So I brought them home; prepared some snack and refreshments and insisted they stay for lunch. My parents were very upset when they came home and found all those people. Especially when they found out who those people were and where they had come from. They took me a side and threatened to punish me later on for such an irresponsible act. I agreed that I deserved to be punished but first I asked if my mom could teach me how to make a delicious soup so I could feed that hungry group. My mom, who knew me well enough to know I would not give up, stayed with me in the kitchen to make sure I followed her instructions while preparing the soup. Then, I invited my parents to sit and eat with us and to my surprise they warmed up to those students and we all carried out a nice conversation for the rest of the afternoon. Ultimately, I believe, my parents saw little use in trying to control me so they decided to support me with feeding and housing those people for a little while. I even convinced some of our neighbours to support me in helping those students and they did just that. They admired my passion and offered to support me in anyway possible. While my parents and our neighbours were fully aware of adverse consequences of their actions, should the government agents find out about such activities, they did not abandon me or those students.

In school, I was the geek who buried herself in books. When teachers introduced new lessons, I was as still as a monk in a meditative state. Once at home the first thing in my mind, right before I took off my school uniform and before I had my afternoon snack, was to go to my room and get started on my homework. In our busy household it was not easy to find an empty room for studying; so I would choose the room that my mom used for storage to work on my assignments without interruptions. If I needed to memorize something, I would go to our flat roof to study taking advantage of fresh air and uninterrupted time. I needed enough space to pace back and forth and read out loud in order to memorize the material. When I was done with my homework, I would review the new chapters that our teachers planned to cover the next day. And finally, when I was completely done, I would put my books neatly away and run off to play with my friends before dinner. Sometimes if it was not too late in the evening, I would go back to my friends, playing, until it was time for us to go to bed. That was pretty much my daily routine. I was always happy during the school months; however, during summer break, I felt miserable since I missed school, my teachers and my classmates.

Other kids my age, including my siblings, were excited about summer break. Most of them studied to pass the exam and finish the school year successfully. Not too many of those I knew at the time shared the same enthusiasm and love for school as I did. Most parents chased after their children to encourage them to attend to their school work; and sometimes they had to threaten them with future punishments before they successfully got their children to focus on school. My parents however, never had this problem with me.

Perhaps my obsession with books and school emanated from the fact that I had mapped out my life at a young age. I did not care about norms and cultural beliefs that were influencing our people one way or the other. Family, media, friends and peers each had a big role in encouraging people to choose a certain path in life. Nothing could come close to getting in my way as I had a clear vision of what I wanted in life and how to go about getting it. My love for books, school and learning was genuine and it came to me naturally. But I was also aware that doing well in school would be a determining factor in turning my life long dream into a reality. So early in life, I knew I would be a university professor; and I was taking action according to that vision.

CHAPTER 3 –
1979 IRAN'S REVOLUTION

Ideology separate us…dreams and anguish brings us together…
(Unknown source)

****

At the time of Iran's so called revolution, in1978/79, I was 13. Before the revolution, Iran's government was an absolute Monarchy. Our king, Shah Pahlavi, who ruled the country for nearly four decades, fled the country along with his family; and the Islamic democratic regime, under Ayatollah Khomeini's leadership, was formed.

When Khomeini first arrived, he assured everyone that regardless of people's gender, age or their political or religious beliefs, everyone would be entitled to their basic human rights, their freedom. He declared that Iran was going to be run by a regime built by its people and for its people. He promised Iranians that the religious leaders were not going to be involved in politics or take part in running the country in any way. Slowly but surely, most Iranians noticed a huge difference between what was promised and what was taking place in our country. A short while after Khomeini officially formed his new government the terror and bloodshed started again; only this time it was in the name of God and Islam. The government was defending its position without offering an explanation or apology for the killing spree. This is my understanding of what the new regime claimed they intended to do in Iran. They claimed

17

they were forming a democratic government with well defined rules to look after everyone's best interest. Disagreeing with the religion and government officials meant starting a war with God. Putting it simply I only saw one rule; defiance would justify severe consequences such as heavy financial penalties, imprisonment, torture, or death! Those who fought God's representatives, the new dictators, would be executed. And those who took part in capturing and killing members of opposition groups had guaranteed a spot in heaven for themselves because of doing the God's work on earth.

Unlike what the government had promised, equality was just an empty word; and our media, TV, Newspapers, and Radio were heavily censored. Another broken promise was the financial abundance that was promised to us by sharing the profit from selling Iran's oil. And since the new dictators stopped at nothing to silence the opposition, not too many people dared to speak up against them. The government leaders claimed to be God's soldiers on earth; so they expected people to obey their orders without question.

Women were the first group affected by the new rules. They were treated as a second class citizen and not equal to men. They were forced to cover their hair and their bodies with a thick, dark, long cover, called Chador. Women could only wear make up while in their homes but were not allowed to have make up on outside of their homes. They were no longer free to apply for their subjects of interest at the university if that subject was considered to be proper only for men. Women lost their right to divorce their spouse if the marriage was not working, except under very special circumstances. Worst of all, divorced women would lose custody of their children as the new law was automatically granting full custody to men. This was perhaps one of the biggest reasons why women tolerated the intolerable in their marriages. As well, men were given permission to marry four women legally and have many more temporary marriages; in Farsi this was called Sigheh. This was another type of discrimination against women, since they could no longer enjoy secure and sacred relationships with the assurance that men would not go outside of their marriages. Living inside such a deep, dark and scary grave, dug by the government, was smothering women. They were enraged by such unjust treatments but did not have the power to do anything about it. Chaos, bloodshed, rage and fear had cast an ugly shadow on our very existence. Most people felt lost and powerless.

It was about this time that my parents had come back from their 30-day trip to Mecca (Makah). Traditionally, when someone came back from such trips, in Islam considered holy trips, family and friends would come for a visit. There would be days and nights of celebration which translated into large family lunches, dinners and gatherings. Our house was no different. It was always crowded as many of our relatives, who lived in or outside of Tehran, came for a visit. Some of them stayed with us for several days or weeks before returning to their homes. I loved having people around and I remember coming home from school everyday excited to find our relatives in our home. As well, I was excited to see my father at home, since he was retired by that time. He always had great stories to tell us and since he was a great story teller, I was always eager to spend time with him. This time I was more excited since he had many interesting things to share regarding their trip to Mecca. When he talked about Mecca, his face was glowing and there was sincerity in his tone that pulled me in more than ever. One of his first stories was about a series of rituals they had to participate in during their stay in Mecca which was called Hajj. My father explained that during Hajj hundreds of thousands of people were to walk seven times about the Ka'bah, the cube-shaped building which acts as the Muslim direction of prayer; kiss the Black Stone in the corner of the Ka'bah; run back and forth between the hills, drink water from the Zamzam well, which is inside the Great Mosque, pray at the Station of Abraham, sacrifice an animal, usually a sheep or a goat and distribute the meat between the poor, throw pebbles at three spots where Satan is believed to have tempted the Prophet Ismail and spend a night in the open at Muzdalifah, near Mecca. I was fascinated. When I finally went to bed, I remember dreaming about Mecca.

My aunt, who accompanied my parents on this trip, displayed the same enthusiasm and zest when she shared her stories. My mom quietly smiled as she listened in to my aunt's stories but she was the only person who was quiet and did not look too energetic. She was pale and looked as though she had aged ten years during her thirty day stay in Mecca. At first I thought it was the hot weather in Saudi Arabia that had made her a bit sick. Then I thought that perhaps being away from her children, especially her baby daughter, had not agreed with her. But after listening to my parents' conversation I found out that my mom was very ill. I heard that prior to their departure to Saudi Arabia, she had discovered a lump in her breast. However, she decided not to cancel her trip and to visit a specialist after her return. This trip was too important to my mom. She was a religious person who had looked forward to this holy trip for years. Besides, she was young and always healthy so she was not too concerned. However, while in Mecca her pain had worsened to the point that if anyone touched her left arm by accident it triggered an unbearable pain. My aunt shared that during her stay in Mecca she and my dad had to be my mom's personal bodyguards to ensure no one got too close to her. According to what I had heard about Hajj, I could imagine how difficult it was for my mom to participate and perform those rituals without being squeezed. But luckily my dad and aunt were successful in helping my mom complete Hajj. That made my mom very happy as her life long dream had finally come true.

I still did not think that there was anything serious going on with my mom, but I was glad that she was back to see a specialist for a complete check up. I believe my mom was booked for an urgent appointment with her doctor shortly after her arrival. Our life was never the same after that visit.

One day I came home from school to find my parents, my aunts, uncles and even my cousins crying as if someone had died. I nervously asked everyone what was wrong and finally found out that my mom's visit with her doctor had not gone well. She had been scheduled for emergency surgery and was leaving for the hospital immediately. Though I believed nothing bad could ever happen to my mom, at this point I felt apprehensive. Since I did not want to let any negative thoughts in, I tried to look at things from a more positive perspective. I thought about my mom, who was almost 43 at a time, as a young, healthy and spiritual person who had her whole life ahead of her; not to mention a gorgeous 18-month old baby girl who was practically inseparable from her. My mom never drank in her life nor did she ever smoke; and she always followed a healthy diet. She attended to people who were really poor and offered her services, as a midwife, for free to pregnant women who could not afford to go to hospital to deliver their babies. All of my mom's patients, her friends, her family and even all of her in-laws truly loved her. I was convinced that God will protect such a person and her young family. On the other hand, I had no concept of death; more so I though it was unfair that young people died especially those with children.

It was hard to believe that at that young age, 13, not only had I to witness the chaos and bloodshed in my country, but now my siblings and I had to watch our mom endure such agonizing physical and emotional pain. Our worst nightmare had come true. She was diagnosed with breast cancer and doctors thought that it was a bit late to do much about it. Of course we, the youngest children, did not know how serious my mom's illness was since my father did not share many details with us. I believe my father tried to protect us as much as possible. But it was only too obvious to see that something was very wrong. My mom was never the same after she came back from her surgery. She suffered every minute of every day. I watched her go through unbearable pain, in and out of hospitals, through much draining and painful radiation and chemotherapy sessions. I felt helpless and terrified as I realized there was nothing I could do to help out. So I cried. And I cried some more. I cried during the day when no one was around and I cried at night when I was supposed to be sleep. I never cried in front of my family or friends but as soon as I found some time alone, I cried. I cried when I saw my mom crying. I could not imagine that I might lose my mom.

My mom's grief and tears were from the physical pain she was enduring and because she feared for our future in case she did not survive. She was a nurse so she was fully aware of the symptoms and stages of her disease. Her awareness and anticipation of what was ahead intensified her pain and suffering that much more. My mom was devastated at the thought of leaving us behind, especially her 18-month old baby. She had asked my father and us to spend more quality time with my 18-month old sister thinking that this would protect her daughter from further suffering. She thought that if anything happened to her, my baby sister would already detached from her to some degree and closer to us instead. The more my mom kept distant from my baby sister, the more she demanded to be with her. She intuitively knew something was wrong.

Living under such circumstances and witnessing such painful family drama felt like a slow and torturous death to me and I am sure my siblings felt the same way. However, for some strange reason we were never able to share our pain or talk about it openly. Though we were a close family, we did not know how to share our sorrow. Perhaps each one of us tried to appear strong so as to protect the other in the family. Or perhaps silence was our coping strategy in such a tragic circumstance. But our self-imposed silence spoke of our grief much louder than words could ever do. Even in complete silence, if someone took the time to sit and truly listen to us, they could see that we were all in pain.

I still remember my baby sister's sad eyes when she looked at my mom with disappointment. She was such a special baby. She quietly observed our reactions but rarely cried or asked for much. Though she could feel something was wrong, she still looked puzzled as to why she was being denied the love she craved for so much. She sensed that her mom loved her with every fibre of her being; so she wondered why her mom was pulling away from her. She behaved differently from kids her age. When we held her in our arms and spoke to her, she listened as though she understood all that we said. Perhaps she was trying to understand what was happening but she was just too young to comprehend such tragic circumstances. She was never bored when she was around my mom; and she did not need entertainment when she had my mom by her side. She used to crawl into my mom's arms and hold her tight. She would rest her head on my mom's chest as if she was trying to listen to her heart beat. She would stare at my mom with her big beautiful brown eyes which were filled with sadness and curiosity. No doubt she touched my mom's heart every time she was that close; but at the same time I believe my mom suffered more knowing full well that she did not have much time to spend with her adorable baby and rest of her children. My older siblings mourned in their own way. They never shared their sorrow with the rest of the family and tried to be strong for all of us. Perhaps they intended to protect their younger sisters and brother in their own way. Or maybe they secretly hoped for my mom's miraculous recovery and did not want to focus on harsh realities surrounding her situation too much.

Being a witness to all that was happening within our family was breaking our hearts into pieces. I felt overwhelmed with my pain and the pain and suffering of my family. So I buried myself in my books and did my best to focus on school and my studies. This was my way of finding refuge, to distance myself from the tragedy and turmoil that had found its way into our young family. And as our family was going through this painful drama, a new government was forming in Iran.

At 13, I was the ground breaker in the family. My brothers and sisters were not interested in politics, and they mostly kept their opinions to themselves. But we had one thing in common and that was the fact that each and every one of us were strong willed and free spirited in our own way and none of us acted according to our cultural or societal norms. Perhaps growing up in a family where our parents never dictated their will had something to do with the way we each turned out.

It did not take long for many people in Iran to question their religious beliefs. Some even went so far as to question the existence of God; especially a God whose mission was to destroy his own creation.

I was drawn to religion and truly believed that there has always been a higher power, a creator who is watching over us. Regardless of what was being done in the name of Islam by the new dictators, I still believed in God, the prophets and all religions. I was reading books by Dr. Ali Shariati, an activist who was assumed to be murdered at the hands of Iran's intelligence service in Shah Pahlavi's time. He described Islam in a way that resonated with me. And that is why I became Mujahedeen's supporter, the opposition group that actively fought new dictators. There were some similarities between Mujahedeen's version of Islam and the version described by Dr. Shariati, and I believe that was the biggest reason I was drawn to them. Other opposition groups did not peak my interest since they either had Marxist Leninist ideology or that they did not appear too genuine to me. Though it was really hard for me to believe what was happening in the name of God, I was not willing to accept the claim of the new dictators that this was God's will. It was heartbreaking to witness what was happening to our people. I heard of parents who reported their own children to government agents. I heard of mothers who encouraged their teenage children to fight in the Iran/Iraq war on the front lines of Iran's borders, and throw themselves under army tanks, to get killed and go to heaven. And I knew of people who reported their own friends or neighbours to government agents to take part in God's mission on Earth. There were also people who played the spy to get ahead, not because they believed in the new government.

By now, we were living in an apartment building in Tehran. While we all enjoyed living in a big house, my parents did not like the location that much. So they decided to sell the house and move to an apartment in nicer area of town. We had regular blackouts for hours at a time and emergency power generators in middle class buildings such as ours did not always function properly. One day during the blackout one of our neighbours was going out with her nine-month old baby using the staircase when the blackout happened. She missed some steps and fell. When she got up she noticed that her baby was not crying. Soon she noticed that the baby was no longer breathing. She picked her up, ran back upstairs, and let out a loud scream calling my name. As soon as we heard her, I ran to the door and pulled her in. I did not know how to handle that situation; but luckily my mom and my older aunt were home at the time. They performed CPR on the baby and soon the baby started to breathe again. This was an intense and nerve-racking experience for me. I had never first hand witnessed such an incident and I prayed to God that I never get to see things like this in the future either. I remember quietly praying and hoping for a miracle and thankfully our prayers were answered. Who knows what might have happened if we were not home that day. The young mother, who was in shock, finally came to. It took her a while before she stopped crying. She held her baby closely; kissing her; smelling her and thanking God that she was alive. When she was calm enough to talk, she asked to call her husband and have him come and pick her up. She made the phone call and while waiting for her husband, we made her a nice cup of tea and asked her to sit with us and relax for a bit.

When our neighbour left, I went about my business but I could overhear my mom's conversation with my aunt. Apparently she was concerned about the fact that, at the age of 16, I was the first person our neighbours called upon when in trouble. As I continued to listen to their conversation, I wondered why my mom was reacting that way. After all, I knew my mom as a free spirited, loving and strong woman with a heart bigger than the entire world who had always been eager to help people in need. It was hard for me to understand why she was so concerned to see her daughter behave so much like her.

My parents knew that I behaved more like those who were on the black list of the new dictators. They knew I never dreamed of marrying a handsome man, living in a big house with white fences and raising children. They knew I never gave importance to my appearance that much or followed up on fashion trends. They could see a sparkle in my eyes every time I saw an opportunity to offer lending hands to people less fortunate than us. They knew how passionate I was about life and how far I would go to get what I wanted. Yes I was different. I had big dreams.

I was an honours student almost all of my school years from grade one to my high school years. This was neither to buy my parents' approval nor to feel important among my classmates; I just truly enjoyed learning and absolutely loved school. Sitting in the class and listening to my teachers felt like a meditation session to me. That was a place I felt absolute joy and peace; a place that no negative thought, worry or fear could ever exist. My classroom was my safe space where no one could interrupt my happy and purposeful existence. While I was in the classroom, listening to lectures, reading books, and learning something new was all that I thought about. I was happiest when school was open in September and I was the most miserable during the summer holidays. Though I had a great many friends and cousins to keep me entertained and occupied, I would miss school terribly. Perhaps I was apprehensive because I had a strange feeling that I might lose all that meant everything to me.

I had decided that I would become a doctor in sociology, philosophy or social psychology and teach at the University of Tehran. Ever since I was a little girl that was all I dreamed about. And when I played make believe games, with my friends, all that I wanted to do was play school. I had a small blackboard and some colourful chalk and I was always the loving and passionate teacher. This was more than a make believe game for me. It was more like a sneak preview of what my life looked like when I grew up. The other end of my fantasies, when I was alone in bed trying to get to sleep, was to picture myself transformed into a beautiful young princess. She had long black hair, kind loving eyes, a warm passionate heart and a welcoming smile. Right next to her, me, walked a handsome prince and together we traveled to far far lands to help less fortunate people. Never, in my dreams, did I see myself wearing expensive jewellery or even a crown; nor did I see myself in the company of people with great wealth and status. Instead, in my fairy tale fantasy I saw that as my prince and I arrived to a city, we brought so much light and laughter to people who looked pale and in pain. We then held their hands, touched their hearts and made their pain go away.

Within a couple of years, and soon after the new dictators solidified their power, people noticed a huge discrepancy between what was promised and what was actually taking place. The very purpose of the revolution in Iran was to put an end to repression. Yet we soon realized that we were moving from a monarch dictator to a religious one. A democratic system and social equality were promised, yet tyranny was what we got in the end. A year or two after the revolution, most political groups started to organize movements against the new regime. Opposition parties wanted to raise awareness among the young and educated at universities, colleges and high schools. They were also counting on students to help them distribute newspapers, books and tapes among people in different parts of the city.

It is not too difficult to guess I was one of the many students who was drawn to these groups. I soon became a supporter of the Islamic opposition group named Mujahedeen. I think I became attracted to this group since they claimed to be the advocate for freedom and democracy. As well, they fundamentally believed in God and Islam, but they had such a different spin on religion, that made it look quite interesting to me! I read their newsletters and books and attended their group meetings in school to learn about their perspective on how to stand up for our beliefs. All opposition parties claimed they were fighting for freedom and our basic rights as human beings. And all of them condemned dictatorship and tyranny. Yet each group had its unique philosophy about the universe and higher power; and they each perceived life slightly different from others. I resonated with Mujahedeen the most considering that they spoke of Koran the way Dr. Shariati did. At the same time, they were not religious fanatics which sat well with me since I believed there were many ways of getting to the same truth. In other words, I always believed that people could peacefully live together regardless of how much they differed in their beliefs. I was convinced that I wanted to work with them, and to be involved in the process of raising people's awareness. I wished to be among those who risked their lives to inspire others to fight for their freedom. I did not believe that politically motivated massacres, under the false name of Islam, were paving our way to Democracy! And so I acted on my beliefs. I talked to my friends and classmates in school to get them to question their beliefs about our new government. I entered debates and passionately talked about my beliefs and ideals about democracy and freedom. Of course, as a supporter of Mujahedeen, I encouraged other students to take the time and read some newsletters and books. I knew that would not sit well with government agents but I had no idea of how far they would go to silence those whose only crime was to speak up.

Chapter 4 -
War between Iran and
Iraq (1980-1988):

"In war, truth is the first casualty." -Aeschylus (Dan Thanks)

****

Regardless of the uncertain and stressful environment surrounding us, life had to go on. People were forced to find a way to cope with their frustrations. Less than two years into our so called Islamic revolution, the senseless war between Iran and Iraq started. Many people believed that the only purpose of that war was to defuse the internal opposition and redirect people's attention to a more serious threat at hand. The war definitely bought all Iranians together, including the opposition parties, since they all shared one common enemy. This detracted attention from the political prisoners who were being tortured at the hands of the new dictators; and kept people quiet so they would tolerate the intolerable.

Most religious fanatics and poor people who never got proper schooling were brain washed into believing that joining forces with soldiers in that war would pave their way to heaven. There were line ups of untrained civilians who volunteered to join the army. After all, they were promised that if they died in the war, they would go straight to heaven. And as difficult as it is to believe, some families looked forward to hearing that their loved ones had made the front line, regardless of the fact that they were never properly trained. Some went so far as to hope that someday they would hear the news of the loved one who got killed in the war. They believed their loved ones would go straight to heaven just as soon as they were killed. Once there, they would ensure a space in heaven for the rest of the family. Our government had promised to take good care of their survivors. Life then became a whole lot better for families who had lost a loved one in the war. They would automatically be enrolled into a program of generous financial assistance on a regular basis. A survivor's family member would have the guaranteed admission to Iran's best universities. Finding a desirable job would no longer be a problem for families who had lost their loved ones in the war.

Who paid the price in this senseless war? Mothers who lost their sons; wives who lost their husbands; children who lost their fathers; sisters who lost their brothers; innocent people who lost their lives, and those were buried alive when our cities were being bombed by the Iraqi air force.

Those who were not getting killed in the war, whether as soldiers or as civilians, were being brutally tortured and murdered at the hands of their own countrymen in prisons. The real tragedy was all that was happening in the name of God! Perhaps this is not such an uplifting comparison but at least those who lost their loved ones in the war could look forward to getting their bodies back for proper goodbye and burial. But families, whose loved ones were executed in prisons, seldom got their bodies back. And on a rare occasion that a family was permitted to collect the lifeless body of their loved ones, they had to pay enormous amount of money to purchase it. No one from the extended family or close friends was allowed to attend the funeral or visit the family to offer condolences. Their graves could not have a tombstone, and if one was erected, it was torn down the next day. Those who were stubborn enough to ignore such rules would mysteriously disappear or would have an unfortunate accident happen. The family of deceased political prisoners did not have a chance to enter university or apply for government jobs regardless of their qualifications.

Cemeteries were full of graves with broken tombstones. Government agents kept an eye on family or friends wanting to visit the grave and forcefully removed them from the cemetery. The government had denied all those killings. So they could not afford media attention to that many bodies piling up at the cemetery. Media in Iran clearly did not have freedom to publish such news, but the government knew if the opposition parties get hold of this information, they would publish it in their own privately run papers, flyers and books. Also, the Iranian government feared this news would travel internationally so they were absolutely determined to keep it contained. When we watched TV or listened to news on the radio, it was announced that another drug dealer or thief was sentenced to death and executed. However, the vast majority of our people did not buy such stories. We knew those unfortunate souls were actually our friends, family members and neighbours whose only crime was speaking up. But the more people feared the government and stayed quiet, the more the bloodshed continued. By squeezing the life out of our very existence, the new regime was becoming stronger and more in control with every passing day. As a result, chances of survival or freedom for those who were being tortured in prisons became slimmer. People feared that they were being listened to when using the phone. They were terrified to trust anyone fearing they were being watched at work or in school. Iran's postal service was also affected. On many occasions letters and packages mysteriously disappear and would not get to their intended recipients. The intelligence service in Iran reserved the right to open any envelope, parcel or package if they were suspicious of something, which was almost all the time. People watched what they said even in their own family gatherings; no one knew who was listening to them and who was working as a spy for the government. Iranians who were living outside of Iran could not receive accurate information about the situation. They feared for the safety of their family and friends. To cope with such unbearable circumstances, people joked about the severity of repression in Iran. If two friends who had not seen one another for a while got together and talked about matters of personal nature, like their love life or potential plans to have children in the near future, they would sometimes say things like this: "well as far as I know, no marriage or babies in the picture in the near future, but to be on the safe side let's check with the government agents to confirm this information".

Life was not easy. It appeared we were fighting a losing battle. Trying to bear the unbearable and surviving the intolerable circumstances seemed like an impossible mission. No longer were we able to feel and breathe the fresh air. Instead we smelled blood and fear everywhere we turned. It was no longer possible to enjoy the beautiful bright sun and its warmth as the dark clouds of pain and misery were blocking the way. The beautiful blue sky appeared red. It was as if the blood shed in our country had reached up so far to have touched the sky! People rarely laughed or even smiled. Instead they let out long and painful sighs as they grieved their losses. As we walked along streets and alleys, we could see large frames with pictures of young men who had lost their lives it the war. Most of the frames were decorated by red tulips and lots of candles to honour their memory. From the distance, if we listened carefully, we could hear the heartbreaking sobbing of mothers', sisters', daughters' and wives. Grieving women covered in black, head to toe, pale and in pain. They appeared as though they did not have much life left in them.

CHAPTER 5 -
THE NIGHT OF MY ARREST:

"Life is drawing without an eraser!!!" (Unknown Author)

****

Horror and anguish finally forced its way into our young family when doctors told my mom that she literally did not have much time to live; she was almost 48 years old. They recommended that my mom be transferred to hospital so they could try to manage her pain with morphine and other heavy duty pain killers. We, the younger children, still did not fully understand what going back to the hospital meant. We had no idea about my mom's prognoses or what the doctors had discussed with my father and older sisters. After all, over the past four years she had gone to the hospital many times and had come back to us each time.

We all helped our mom get ready for the hospital. We packed a small bag for her and soon she was ready to go. Then, our family planned round clock shifts of those of us at home who could stay at the hospital for emergency purposes. I was given a late night shift as I had the ability to stay up all night if I wanted to. Though I was 16 at the time, I was too naive to understand how serious my mom's situation was. Instead, I was actually hopeful that she would get well soon.

I was happy to be there for my mom when she needed her family the most. I thought that this would give us a chance to have some private mother-daughter time that I had craved. With work and so many children my mom had little time or energy to interact with us. She always had so much on her plate and was just too exhausted for quality time with her kids. She had a full time job; part time office hours at home for her local patients and she was a full time mother to her six children. We always had guests over. There were either friends and family members in Tehran or our out of town extended family that stayed with us quite frequently for a few weeks to a few months. Managing all that took considerable time and energy on her part, but we, as children, could not really understand that at the time. I must admit that as a child, I took all that personally, and at times, I feared that my mom might not be fond of me. Consequently, I tried to be the "good" child, and that meant growing up much faster than I was supposed to. I felt that I should not ask for much. Instead I tried to be more responsible and behave maturely. Now, as a teenager, I saw my mom in and out of hospitals with a serious illness that drained her body and soul. She had been suffering for several years and had not much left in her. My older sisters were married at the time so they were not available to help out everyday, though they tried their best. I took over most chores around the house and did my best to be there for my younger siblings as much as possible.

Though my dad had an active part in raising the children, and was retired by then, I still missed my mom. I am sure my siblings felt the same way and wished that someday she would be able to spend more time with us. Longing to reconnect with my mom, I thought nights at the hospital would be our uninterrupted times together. I wanted to use that time to let my mom know how much she meant to me. Perhaps I hoped to hear her say that she loved me, and was proud of me just the way I was. My insecurity stemmed from knowing how much she disapproved of my careless actions in supporting Mujahedeen. She was clearly terrified of how far I might go and what the future would hold for me.

While now I have no doubts of my mom's love and affection for me, those days I took her disapproval to mean that I was not fully loved and accepted. Such feelings brought much pain and discomfort which transformed itself into feelings of guilt and apprehension. And that night as I was alone with my mom, I felt more anxious than ever. First and foremost, I was not sure how I could handle seeing my mom in such excruciating pain and discomfort. Second, I was afraid to find out how my mom truly felt about me. I was consumed by so many fearful thoughts and much more untamed emotions. It took everything I had within me to hide my inner turmoil so my mom would not pick up on it. After all, I wanted her to be hopeful and focused on healing not to add to her worries or concerns. Fate had something different in store for us.

Before sharing what happened to me next, I would like to take you back in time to take a closer look at circumstances that gave birth to that gloomy night.

In Iran, after the Islamic Regime took power, there were undercover government agents in every school hired as teachers, principals or vice principals. They were spies. Their primary responsibility was to watch, listen and report back any suspicious behaviours or activities within or even outside of school. To gain better control over students and staff, the government spies needed to create a bigger and more reliable network of allies within school. They used some of the students who were willing to be involved in God's work. Many people were only too happy to help redeem sinners; and as such they committed some of the most vicious acts in human history.

I was almost 16 when I was dismissed from school due to my activities with Mujahedeen. Apparently a couple of the spies in my school had recommended my dismissal since I was known as one of Mujahedeen's supporters. They believed that I was adversely influencing other students so they had asked the principal to remove me from school. The principal knew my parents so she called them for a meeting immediately. My mom was not well so my dad went to school to meet with the principal. During the meeting she had advised my father of what was happening and asked that he find a new school for me effective immediately. She had told my father that this was not an easy decision for her but this ultimately was for my own good. I remember how upset my father was when he got home that day. My mom was outraged with what she heard later on as well. Both of them came down pretty hard on me and ordered me to stay away from Mujahedeen once and for all. When my father shared the outcome of his meeting, I found out that I could no longer go back to my high school. He informed me that he had found another high school not too far from where we lived and had already registered me there. I was devastated to hear this news but knew that I had no choice but to act in accordance with my parents and my principal's decision. Besides, I was in grade 12 so I knew I only had to stay in that school for a year. I had accelerated in my studies and had finished grade 10 and 11 in one school year; so now at 16, I was starting grade 12.

While I was really sad to be away from my closest friends, those I had known for almost a decade, it did not take me too long to find few new good friends. I also managed to connect with those who, like me, spoke up and expressed their political beliefs. Very soon I got noticed again. Teachers and students who were in fact undercover agents labelled me as a trouble maker and soon I found myself in a hole bigger than ever. Despite all the odds, the principal who had known me only a short while took a liking to me. She met with me on numerous occasions to caution me about the consequences of my actions, and warned me about what could be waiting for me if I did not stop. I had assured her that she had nothing to worry about as all she had heard was mostly unsubstantiated rumours.

Finally a short while after, of the teachers brought up two names that she thought our principal should deal with immediately. Undoubtedly I was one of the two students she had named. She believed that we were disturbing the peace in our school. The other one was a wonderful girl in my class with whom I had become too close in a short time we had known each other; her name was "Mina". This teacher had indicated that she knew, through her sources, we had books and newspapers that were banned by the government in our possession; and that we were sharing them with other students. In one instance, she had mentioned she had finally caught us in the act, took the newspaper from us, and gave us a warning to stop what we were doing or else! She had labelled us as potential threats that needed to be taken care of immediately. At the same meeting she had mentioned to our principal that her colleagues, spies for the government, would be visiting the school very soon. Our principal was very smart and knew that I was in serious trouble. Later on we found out that she had witnessed such incidents in previous schools where she worked before. She seemed determined to protect her students at any cost and to the best of her ability. Our principal was not a supporter of the new dictators and she cared deeply about her students. Almost immediately she called my father and asked him to take me out of school. She assured him that this was for my own good and my only way out of this serious trouble. She then shared what she had heard from that teacher, the government spy, and her concerns regarding my presence in school. She convinced my father that I was only steps away from prison unless they could send me away for a while and out of sight.

Understandably, my parents were really upset with me when they found out about all this so I was left with no choice but to quit school. My parents' main concern was to keep me safe. My schooling was the second priority for them. Besides, they knew I could easily study at home and write my exams at the board of education to get my diploma. After all, I had done this before. I had studied and passed two grades in one school year. For grade 11, I had only studied three months, during the summer, at home without receiving any tutoring. So my parents were confident that taking me off school would not in anyway interfere with my education.

However, I was restless and unhappy. Part of my love for school was to interact with teachers and students. I truly believed that learning comes mostly from sharing experiences and observation rather than reading books. Besides, that was my chance to leave the house. Now I was not allowed to leave the house too often without my family's supervision; and my friends could not visit me that much either. Spending so much time at home meant witnessing my mom's pain and suffering all day long; and that was draining me from the inside out. With no support and nothing to look forward to, the only thing that kept me going was my books. The anticipation of obtaining my high school diploma and applying for university was all that kept me going.

In those days in Tehran people who chose to, for one reason or another, do home schooling had the option to write their exams at the board of education's head office. The board had set aside designated conference rooms for such purposes. They hire seasonal staff to help with logistics and supervision of those who were writing the exams. Those who passed the tests would receive their certifications by mail within several weeks. Although I was grateful for any opportunity to continue my education, I still struggled with the fact that I was taken away from all of my friends, my teachers and school.

While I was busy studying, the government agents were busy looking for me, and my best friend "Mina" who was also one of Mujahedeen's supporters. My parents thought they had ensured my safety by taking me out of school in time. But they never thought that government agents would go as far as accessing our confidential information, which included our home addresses. In other words, leaving school had only delayed the inevitable.

"Mina" was targeted first. They arrested and tortured her to the point that she finally agreed to help them capture me as well. It was true that they had access to my home address and could come for me anytime, but they did not want to risk dropping by on the off chance that I might not be home. Their strategy made sense; had they come for me and could not get me at home, there was a possibility that I would go into hiding. And since they did not want to take that chance, they had come up with another plan to guarantee my capture. Surrounded by prison guards, "Mina" called home and talked to my father. On the phone, she had indicated that she wanted to find out if I was home so she could come and visit my mom and me. My father did not suspect anything. He knew and trusted "Mina". He informed her that I was staying with my mom at the hospital. She had then asked my father for the name and the location of the hospital so she could visit us that night; and my father provided her with all that information. I found out later on that after my dad hung up the phone, our home was surrounded by quite a few government agents. Several armed men surrounded our building and entered our apartment while simultaneously four others surrounded my mom's hospital room. I was not aware of what was happening at home, and my family had no idea what was going on at the hospital. At some point though, my dad put two and two together. As the agents were busy turning our home inside out, he managed to ask my cousin, who was staying at our home, to call and warn me. He hoped I would have enough time to escape, but unfortunately for all of us, it was just too late.

Back at the hospital, as I was helping my mom get back to her bed from the bathroom, a nurse knocked on the door and asked if she could speak to me outside. All of a sudden, I felt anxious. I could hear my heartbeat and my knees were shaking. Though I did not know why she asked me to leave the room, I had a bad feeling about it. I told my mom that I would be right back and I left the room immediately. As soon as I got to the lobby and saw four men, in civilian clothes carrying large black leather cases, I knew right away what was happening. For a brief moment, I felt as if I was going to have a heart attack as my heart was flying out of my chest. I thought to myself, not here and not now. I was not afraid of what they could do to me but what this could do to my mom! The nurse in charge soon found out who those men were and why they had come for me. She took me aside and asked why I had not given her a heads up about all that. She went on to say that if she had known, she might have been able to refuse them access to our room at least for couple of hours. I thanked her but confessed that I had absolutely no idea of what was coming my way.

While I was going through this horrifying experience, I knew that I had to pull myself together and perhaps come up with a way to protect my mom in anyway possible. So the first thing that came to my mind was to prevent my mom from finding out what was happening outside of her room. I quickly started the negotiation process and calmly explained my mom's situation to those agents. The nursing staff corroborated my story and gently warned them that any additional distress might put my mom into a state of shock. They provided as much details as they were allowed to so as to ensure those agents were aware of the severity of my mom's situation. Meanwhile, I could hear my mom's voice calling for me and asking where I was and what I was doing for that long. She wanted me back in the room almost as if she was afraid she was going to lose me that night. I could hear her anxiety through her trembling voice and that was breaking my heart into thousands of pieces. I was doing my very best to convince my mom that there was nothing to be concerned about but she sounded absolutely terrified. I was ready to give anything the agents asked for so they would just wait outside of the room and let me stay with my mom for another couple of hours. I was hoping that while I was with my mom she would fall sleep and by the time she was up, one of my siblings would be there to take over my shift. This way, my mom would not suspect anything as she would think that I had gone home to get some sleep to get ready for my next shift. But the agents were not interested in my story nor did they take me or the nurses seriously. Instead, they pointed to their guns and hinted that they were well prepared to take me in forcefully if there was any resistance on my part. It was at that point that I decided to leave with them before I potentially endangered anyone else's life in the process. I turned to one of the nurses on duty and asked her to help convince my mom that I had to leave but that I would be back very soon. Her eyes were tearing up but she reluctantly entered my mom's room and left me alone with the agents. At that point, I asked the agents for their permission to get back to the room to take my purse, make up a story to tell my mom and call home so someone could come and take my shift at the hospital. They reluctantly agreed to let me go back in while they waited outside; but every couple of minutes, one of them would open the door to take a peak just to ensure I was still there. I guess they were afraid that I might jump 22 stories to commit suicide or that I might have been reaching for some sort of weapon that I had hidden in my purse.

Meanwhile, my mom's phone rang. I was hoping it was my family calling to check up on us so I could ask them to get to hospital urgently. It was my cousin in a frantic state telling me to leave urgently before the government agents could get to me. She did now know that I was almost in their custody so I quickly told her what was happening. I ensured her that there was no way out and that they should just send someone else to stay with my mom. I was almost whispering so neither my mom nor the agents behind the door could hear my conversation. However, I am sure my mom heard some of what I said to my cousin as she kept asking me what was happening and why I was leaving. And finally when she noticed one of the agents, as he was peaking inside to scan her room, my mom realized what was happening. She started to cry, constantly calling for God to help us. She was beside herself, telling me that she knew I was being arrested and that I brought all that upon myself and my family. She said that she had warned me about all that before but I just never listened to her. She was, of course, right. It took everything I had in me not to cry; I only said that I was really sorry. I was still not ready to confirm my mom's worst nightmare so I attempted to make up a story to convince her that all was well. I told her that those agents only wanted to ask me few questions about one of my classmates, and that as soon as I answered all their questions I would be back with her right away. I was never a good liar and my mom was a very smart woman. She did not buy my story. My time was up, and I had to leave immediately or risk being dragged out of her room by four armed men. I looked away and told my mom's nurse to please take care of her for me. When I tried to kiss my mom goodbye, she turned her face away from me so I never had a chance to kiss and hug her and say my goodbyes properly. Somewhere deep inside her, she must have known that was the last time she would ever lay eyes on me. She could not find the strength to deal with all that so she never said goodbye to me.

Guilt and regret was eating away at me as I looked at my mom one last time. As I was leaving the room I saw her glancing back at me as if she was saying her goodbyes. She did not say a word yet she said all that she wanted to say to me with her eyes; and I heard it all. Her eyes spoke of the terror, the agony and the pain she was in at that moment. After almost 30 years, I still remember my mom's distressed look as I said goodbye to her. I still remember her eyes. It has been hard to convince myself that my mom forgave me for the pain and suffering I caused her. Perhaps it is because I have yet not yet been able to forgive myself entirely for what I put her through. Part of me died that night. The other part never left my mom's room. The night of my arrest was also the beginning of my horrifying nightmare; one that I did not seem to be able to wake up from.

Half alive, I left the hospital escorted by merciless agents who called themselves God's soldiers. I was still dazed and confused. I felt as if someone had just hit me on the head with a baseball bat. All I could see was my mom's face and her eyes. I was in a state of shock and disbelief and could not feel anything for a while. It took a while before the feeling of anger and hatred started to surface. As I was consumed with anger and guilt, I was unable to cry.

I was placed on a back seat of a van. Two guards sat at the back with me and the other two sat on the front. All the windows on the van were heavily tinted from the inside so I would not be able to see anything. However, as soon as I entered the car, they put a blindfold over my eyes to ensure I would not see where I was being taken to. They tied it up very tightly; so much so that it was hurting my eyes. It was at that moment, for the very first time, that I realized all that was real. I was not dreaming. I could hear my heartbeat. The shock was wearing off and I had to face the reality of my situation. Though I felt apprehensive, I was not afraid for my life. It did not matter to me if I lived or died anymore. The worst thing that could happen to me had already happened. Consumed by much anger and hatred, I started confronting the agents. I told them how I felt about the regime and their followers, namely people like them. I told them that I thought they were blind to take such sadistic actions against their own people. I told them that killing innocent people would not stop others from fighting for their basic human rights. I assured them that most people knew the truth already and someday they would rise against the regime and reclaim their freedom. I defended Mujahedeen and proudly admitted to being one of their supporters. Needless to say, arguing with armed men who could decide if I were to live or die did not help my case. I knew I would be reprimanded for speaking my mind, but by then, I was just too angry to be concerned about that in anyway. There was no way I would want to keep quiet against those who inflicted such agonizing pain to my mom. How could I think about my safety when I was already taken away from the only person I always felt safe with, my mom? I had already lost all that mattered to me. Nothing else made sense anymore.

After a long drive, the van stopped. I found out later that I was being taken to Eshrat Abad Garrison which was one of the major military stations in Tehran. Since I was not allowed to take my blindfold off, the guard had to take a piece of my chador, a black, long cover to cover all of my body excluding my face, so to get me to follow him. He led me through a long corridor and since I had my blind fold on, I could not see anything but my feet. I was hesitant to walk as fast as he wanted me to since I had hit my head against the walls few times already. The guard was rude. He kept nagging at me to walk faster; but I was terrified of falling down, so I tried to ignore him. At times it seemed as if we were walking in circles and that was making me feel very dizzy. Even without the fast and circular movements I was dizzy since the blind fold was putting too much pressure on my eyes.

Later on I heard that this was one of the techniques guards used to ensure prisoners would not get a sense of where they were or where they were going. As well, the guards wanted to get the prisoners to feel more anxious or sick; that would almost guarantee no resistance while transporting new prisoners to their cells. I must admit that their strategy was working. I felt nauseous and dizzy. And considering that I had not slept for almost 24 hours I was not doing too well and felt pretty sick from all those turns and brisk walking. Slowly but surely, fear of what was happening to me and what could be waiting for me was sneaking up on me. I was breathless and my entire body was shivering. It took all that I had in me not to complain or let the guard notice the condition I was in. I was not going to give them the satisfaction of knowing that they were wearing me out that quickly.

After what seemed like a really long walk, we stopped for a bit and I assumed that we had reached our destination. The guard asked me to enter a room and as I entered the room, I heard a heavy metal door closing behind me. I was told that I could take off my blindfold when the door was closed. I immediately too it off and that was my first chance to glance at my cell which looked like a solitary confinement cell. Only I saw that I was not alone in there. In a small cell that was designed for one person, they had locked up three other girls in addition to me. They said hi to me while staring at me with curiosity and noticeable apprehension. I had always greeted people with a smile and I was not about to make an exception that night either. Regardless of the physical and emotional condition I was in, I said hi to them with a smile and introduced myself. Looking more curious, my cellmates smiled back and introduced themselves. I immediately asked if they knew where we were and they responded by saying that we were being held in Eshrat Abad Garrison. They did not expect such a peaceful encounter with someone who had just been thrown in prison. Apparently most prisoners entered their cell kicking, screaming and crying. I now knew why my cellmates looked astonished when they first saw me. Behind their smile though, there was a cloud of sadness for they had to witness the imprisonment of yet another young girl. They were warm and friendly and they quickly made me feel welcomed. As soon as the introduction was over, I asked if I could first say my prayers as I had not been able to do so when I was at the hospital.

I was born a Muslim but only consistently said my prayers for the past couple of years. The reason I enjoyed saying prayers was that I would immediately feel peaceful and centered. Through my prayers I would get to speak to God and feel his presence right there with me. I felt stronger, more connected and purposeful when I spoke to God during my prayers.

With utter amazement those girls gave me their blessings to go ahead with my prayers and so I did. When I was finished, I felt calmer; as if a warm shower ran through my entire body. My new friends could no longer hold back so they started questioning me to find out who I really was, why I was arrested and to what degree I was involved with the opposition party I was supporting. I replied to all of their inquiries with honesty as I felt I was among those who had chosen to speak up for what they believed. It was then their turn to share their sorrowful stories. I listened to their spoken and unspoken words to grasp the depth of their tragedies.

When the initial questioning and sharing was over, they gave me a big hug and told me how happy they were to share their cell with me. As much as I felt that I had gained their trust, part of me sensed that they had not believed my story in its entirety. I had indicated that I had just been reading banned books and newspapers, and verbally supported Mujahedeen's position against the government. Yet, they were looking at me as though I was one of the lead freedom fighters who had been arrested with some sort of weapon on a street fight or something similar to that affect. When I told them how I got arrested they doubted my story, not the part about my mom of course, but the level of my involvement with Mujahedeen. Perhaps my calm and pleasant demeanour had led them to believe that there was more to my story than I was willing to share at the time.

Yet the truth remained that I was just as fearful and devastated as they were; only I could not allow myself to break down and fall into pieces. Perhaps if I were in their place I would not have believed my story either. However, at that time, I had more important concerns; I was worried about my mom and even more worried about my 5-year old sister. After my mom, I was the closest to my baby sister. Now that neither of us was home, I was sure she was distressed. I tried not to let negative thoughts in. I wanted to believe that my family and I were going to be reunited soon. I could never imagine that I might not get to see my family again nor did I ever imagine experiencing such tragedies so early in life.

The universe had something else in store for me. I did not go back to my family the next day; worst, I did not get to see my mom ever again.

Chapter 6 -
Events on the First
3 Weeks of My
Imprisonment-And
Description of My Cell:

"In the depths of winter, I discovered in me an invincible summer."
(Albert Camus 1881-1973)

****

My cell was very small; it only had one small window close to the ceiling, perhaps the size of a legal size paper. This cell was originally built for one person; the room was about 10 by 15 feet. Since they were arresting too many people at a time, they were putting four or five people in one cell. Perhaps that was yet another way to further humiliate and torture us.

Our cell was in a long and narrow hallway that held about 7 or 8 other individual cells. I wondered if there were more cells in other areas of the building; but none of us ever got to see outside of the dark hallway in to confirm that. The cells did not have bars; instead they were built with solid heavy metal doors preventing us from seeing what was happening in the hallway. Lucky for us, or perhaps not, there was a small crack in our door close to the door handle that looked more like a thin line running across the door. So from time to time we could peak to see a little of what was going on outside of our cell. Of course, we would only glance when we could not hear the guards outside. Unfortunately for us, if anyone was standing in the hallway, they could see us peeking as well. My cellmates were careful; however, on a couple of occasions, they were caught and punished. Being beaten by heavy cables was the price they paid for disobeying.

Still, many of us took our chances and used every opportunity to look outside to find out about other prisoners. We saw new prisoners at the time of their arrest and witnessed how they were being treated. We witnessed them dragged and beaten. Before they were thrown into their cells, the guards kicked them many times with their heavy army boots. Sometimes they got hit on the head, chest or back by machine guns if they resisted. We could easily hear prisoners in other cells, especially if they talked out loud, cried, or screamed. We always heard a cry at night and sometimes during the day. Some cried because of their physical pain after being beaten; some cried because they just could not accept being separated from their loved ones; and some cried because they needed to use the washroom urgently, but no one was around to let them out. All and all, it was heartbreaking to see and hear all that was happening outside of our small cell. To this day, I have not forgotten a man's voice sobbing one night. We could tell that he was an older gentleman. We wondered what had happened to him that caused him such pain and agony; yet we never found out about him. I remember another man who sang a very sad song when the lights were off and the guards were not around. It was disheartening to hear such profound sorrow and grief in his voice. I still remember that song and when I hear it somewhere, I feel overpowered by sadness. On those occasions I think about him, praying he survived the prison.

One night, I almost got caught peeking. I was curious to find out who else was out there beside my cellmates and me. As I was fighting the urge to get up and look through the cracked door, I heard a loud scream. I rushed towards the door to see what was happening. I saw a young man getting punched, kicked and dragged into his cell. Apparently, he had just been arrested and he was resisting. The guards gave him a good beating before they threw him inside his cell, making sure that he learned his lesson. As I was too busy figuring out what was happening, I did not hear a prosecutor passing by our cell. As soon as I saw him, I quickly turned around and sat very close to my friends. But it was too late. He had already seen me peeking. He immediately shouted at us to get away from the door and cover ourselves with our chadors so he could enter our cell. As he forced his way in, we all held our breaths. While he was shouting and cursing at us, he asked that the one who was peeking come forward. The room was so quiet we could hear a pin drop. Since none of us spoke up, he threatened to beat all of us. I could not accept that three other people would be beaten because of me. I admitted that I was the one. Before he could say anything, I continued to talk. I told him that I was not aware of all of the rules since I had been arrested only the night before. Of course, this was not true. I had actually been warned about all of this. I told him that since I heard loud noises I automatically, and only for a quick second, looked outside before my cellmates could warn me to move away from the door. And I promised this would never happen again. He was furious at me, still threatening to give all of us a good beating so next time we would think twice about non-compliance.

My cellmates were very frightened. So I told the prosecutor that he should just take me in as they had nothing to do with this. He was surprised to hear my determined voice. He paused for a minute. He opened the door, and on his way out he said, that he'd let this go, only this time, but if this were to happen ever again we would all be in serious trouble. As we heard the heavy door closing behind him, we crawled into each other's shivering arms. I was relieved to know that my cellmates did not endure physical and emotional pain because of my careless act that night.

At the end of the hallway, there was only one small bathroom. This bathroom was really a dark, dirty and scary hole. It was for all the prisoners occupying those 7 or 8 cells. If anyone needed to use it, they had to call the guards. If the guards were around, and could hear our voice, we would get to use the bathroom; but we had to wait our turn. If anyone had to use the bathroom urgently they were in trouble if the guards were not around, or if the bathroom was already occupied. And there were certain times of the night and day that we could not use the bathroom at all since the guards were on a break, or they were dealing with an "emergency" somewhere else in the building. The good news was that to use the bathroom, we did not have to put our blindfolds on. Instead, for a brief moment, the guards would cover their head and face with a large black cloth long enough to get to their shoulders. That mask looked more like a winter hat younger children wore to keep their face, forehead, chin and cheeks covered. Their mask, though, had no other openings except for the eyes; and the guards looked very frightening.

Taking a shower was another traumatic experience for all of us. Following their humiliating rituals was yet another way we were being tortured. On a day that we girls, were scheduled to take a shower, we would pack our bags, put our blindfolds on and wait for the guards. We were then escorted to one of the public showers close to Eshrat Abad Garrison. Public showers were commonly used in Iran at that time. We were put on a bus, with few armed guards. Due to time and space constraints, and to cause us further humiliation, they would put all the prisoners who shared a cell in one shower stall with one shower head. In our case, the four of us were put in a stall with an armed guard outside of the door. We only had a certain amount of time to finish showering, and they threatened to have the water cut off if we were not done in time. Most girls, including me, had long hair, so it was really difficult to get washed and cleaned up in such short time. My cellmates shared that on previous occasions the guards had threatened to get in the shower and throw them out naked if they were delayed. Of course, the girls were terrified, so they would cry and beg for a bit more time. I found out later on that the male prisoners were being treated as sadistically as the women on the scheduled shower days. I even heard that on few occasions, the guards had actually entered the booths and beaten up the naked men who had refused to come out still covered with soap. Taking a shower in front of other prisoners was extremely uncomfortable for all of us. And the fear of being further violated by the guards made things even more dreadful. But there was no way out for us.

It was obvious that these humiliations were part of the plan to tear the prisoners apart and to cause them to question their own sanity. Unfortunately, their strategy was working. We constantly heard loud sobbing and crying. That was the first time in my life that I had heard men cry. It was tough to keep still and not react. No matter how hard I tried to pull myself together and stay strong, all that was getting to me. I had never been that terrified in my life.

Gradually, my cellmates filled me in on all that I needed to know about the rules and the routines of our prison. I learned when breakfast, lunch and dinner were served and how we would receive them. I was informed of daily interrogation schedules. We were to be called in by the prosecutors on the day of our arrest so to take care of preliminary paperwork. However, if it was late at night or very early in the morning, those sessions would be postponed to the next day according to prosecutors' availability. I was cautioned about the unpredictability of how those sessions might go; and that there was always a possibility that anyone of us might come back with bloody feet, a bruised body or a swollen face. That evening I was finally called. I could hear my heart beating. I put my blindfold on, and along with my friends, moved away from the door and faced the wall. When we gave the go ahead that we were ready for the guard to enter our cell, he came in and took me with him. He was harsh and aggressive. While he held on to my Chador to lead me to the office, he purposely walked too fast. I kept hitting my head against the concrete walls. I had no way of protecting myself as I was out of balance because of the blindfold. The narrow spiral hallways were working against me as well. I felt nauseous, dizzy and in pain. Our walk which felt like a lifetime. We finally stopped, and I was told to enter an office. I was almost out of breath. I had been dragged at such a fast speed while my eyes were tightly covered. My fear was slowly rising inside me. I felt helpless. I was trembling. It was late in the evening, and I was all alone. I dreaded the harsh treatments my friends had warned me about. I was glad my face was covered so perhaps I could hide my fear a bit longer. After the way I had responded to the agents who arrested me the night before, I fully expected retaliation. Admitting that I was one of the Mujahedeen's supporters was very damaging to my case. In their eyes, I admitted I was a criminal. As I was preoccupied with my own thoughts, the prosecutor in charge of my case finally walked in. I was facing the wall. He asked me to take off my blindfold. I was informed that I needed to respond to some written questions before we officially started our session. I was advised neither to turn around, nor to move from where I was seated if I did not want to get beaten. As angry as I was of him, and everyone else involved in that prison, I was not even contemplating breaking his rules at that moment. I took off my blindfold and saw a small desk with a pen, and a few pieces of paper in front of me. The prosecutor paused briefly to allow me to get situated and started to talk again. From his voice, I could tell that he was very young.

He wanted me to fear him. He was standing so close I could feel him breathing on my neck. That kind of proximity made me uncomfortable. From what I had heard from my cellmates about him, he was rude, condescending and rough and I could not predict what he might do to me if I got him angry. I was hoping I could control my temper and behave properly, at least throughout the session. All kinds of thoughts were running through my head. I was still unable to grasp the idea that it was okay for someone like me to be arrested just because of what I chose to believe. It was hard for me to hide how disgusted I was with our new regime and its advocates; and I was appalled to see what the new dictators were doing to our people. By the same token, I could understand why people like me posed a threat to the new dictators. People who were against dictatorship and vicious killings and torture under the name of Islam undermined their power. Government officials knew only too well that once people were aware of the crimes committed against them, under the name of God and religion, they would stand up to them and end such corruption.

While I was deep in thought, he started to talk to me in a loud voice. He called people like me criminals who deserved to be punished for declaring war against God and his soldiers. He called us bad seeds that should be stopped at any cost for the good of our country. As much as I disliked him and what he stood for, we both had something in common. Just like me, he seemed very confident that what he believed was the only truth and nothing but the truth! He believed that the new dictators were true advocates of Islam. I was convinced that people should be free to choose their own beliefs without fear of retribution. What I called politically motivated massacres, he called doing God's work on earth. In another place and time we might have had a spirited debate. Obviously, that was wishful thinking. Coming together and agreeing on things was not on his agenda. He was the vicious prosecutor and I was a sixteen year old prisoner who thought she could change the world!

The interrogation continued. Somehow I managed not to direct my anger toward him but to focus on the issue at hand. At times, when I was busy writing, he would come closer, bend forward and lean over my shoulders to read some of what I had written. I could hear him chuckling quietly as though he found some of my answers amusing. One thing was for sure, he now knew I could not lie. There were quite a few pages to go through and many questions to answer. I felt overwhelmed since most of the questions were heading toward one thing; the level of my involvement with the Mujahedeen. I was also asked to name everyone, friends, classmates, neighbours or family members, who at some point had supported them. Some questions were too vague and some more detailed. It was easier to answer to the more general questions such as why I supported the Mujahedeen; but more detailed questions meant giving up names, dates, locations and so on. I had trouble making up names, false dates, and locations, so it took me a long time to get through it all. I admitted taking part in a couple of rallies organized by the Mujahedeen against the government; but said I was there on my own and did not know anyone else.

By now I could tell he had me figured out. He knew that he was talking to an idealist dreamer who was just too young and innocent to know what she was doing. I did not have real facts to share, but I had a lot of feelings. He seemed a bit calmer now. Perhaps he heard the sincerity in my voice. All that worked in my favour as he had become less impatient. I no longer felt as fearful being alone with him. This was such a peculiar situation. A vicious prosecutor feared by prisoners was not, for now, living up to his reputation. I was sure I had escaped a beating, at least that day. I started to breathe easier, but by the same token, I could sense that he was still frustrated with me. I would not come to my senses, so to speak. As I continued to write, I would stop from time to time to respond to his verbal questions, and then go back to working on my papers again. He finally stopped our conversation; asked me to finish writing so I could get ready to be taken back to my cell. When I confirmed that I was done, he took the papers and called a guard to come and collect me. While we waited for him to arrive, he told me that he thought I was just too immature and naïve to know what I was talking about. He went on to say that he thought spending sometime in prison would teach me a lesson. I was quiet for the first time. I felt exhausted and did not want to continue talking. I was only too glad to be dismissed and relieved that I survived my first interrogation.

I could not wait to get back and see my cellmates again. Now that I was away from my family, they were the next best thing to me and I felt safe and comfortable with them. When I finally got back, they welcomed me with open arms. They were anxious to find out how my session went, but happy to see that I did not appear to be beaten. I shared all that had happened. I said my prayers and got ready for bed.

The next morning I woke up to the sound of a very loud cry from another cell in our hallway. When I heard my name in the midst of all that loud noise, I listened even more carefully to find out who was making all that noise. After a few minutes, I recognized the voice of the girl who was sobbing, begging for forgiveness. It was my best friend. She had led the guards to the hospital and eventually to my arrest! I did not know what to say to her, or how to warn her to keep quiet before she was taken away to be beaten up for the commotion she had created. I whispered that there was nothing to forgive, that I did not hold her accountable for all that happened to me. I told her that she was not to blame in any way and anyone else in her place would have broken under torture. I was not sure if she heard or believed a word I said. Her sobbing got louder and louder until finally the guards came and took her. She was very quiet on the way back to her cell. Later, I found out that she had been beaten violently and, in fact, she had been in a very bad emotional and physical state before she finally broke down and helped the guards to locate and arrest me. From that day forward, every time she was being escorted to go to the bathroom, she would whisper my name telling me how sorry she was for what she had done and that she loved me very much. Each time I would respond to her gently that she was already forgiven. Though I could not see her face, I could feel that each time she heard my voice, little bit of the heavy burden she was carrying was being lifted off her shoulders.

It was the third night of my stay when two guards called my name to get ready for yet another interrogation session. It was really late, after the lights were off and we were getting ready for bed. A shiver went through my body, and I felt very uncomfortable to be taken out for an interrogation that late. As I left my cell, I was frightened about what could be waiting for me and wished this was a nightmare I could wake up from now. But somewhere deep inside, I knew this was too real and all this was really happening to me! The routine was pretty much the same. I was blindfolded and pulled quickly through dark and narrow hallways until I reached the office and waited for the prosecutor to enter. I desperately tried to keep cool and not to let these people know how frightened I was. It felt like I had been waiting a lifetime when the prosecutor finally entered the room. He was particularly gentle with me; asking me how I was doing, if I needed to get something to drink. This was the first time he was so caring and that made me feel even more uncomfortable.

In a trembling voice, I responded that I was doing well and assured him that I did not need a drink. He ignored me and pushed a paper cup containing water into my hands insisting that I take a sip before we got started. I decided to listen to him this time, not to make him angry. I drank a bit of water quickly. He then walked toward me, took the cup out of my hands and told me that he was putting the cup next to me on a table in case I needed more water later on. Though I was blindfolded, I was able to see my feet. I could see the table placed very close to me. Next he asked if I wanted to take my blindfold off; he told me that he had no problem putting his mask on. I felt more comfortable with the blindfold on, so I thanked him politely and declined his offer. He then proceeded to tell me that he had just spoken with my father and that he had bad news for me. I was shaking. I felt breathless, but still could not imagine what the bad news could be. He paused for a bit, and with a quiet and sad voice, he announced that my mother had passed away a couple of hours ago. For a moment or two I was completely quiet. I was shocked. I felt I had just been hit on the head by a baseball bat. I was numb, nauseous and dizzy. I was afraid I might fall off my chair. The entire room was spinning at a rapid rate. I covered my mouth as I was afraid I would be sick any minute. It took me quite a while before I could speak. All through that time, the prosecutor sat there with me, quietly. From time to time, he would walk toward me, place a cup in my hands and force me to take a sip. When the initial shock subsided, I told him that my mom cannot be dead; and that he might have had delivered this horrible news to the wrong person. I told him that my mom was at the hospital to receive chemotherapy and go home when that was done.

I said I did not believe him. I wondered if this was his way of torturing me further, so I still held on to some hope that my mom was, in fact, alive. With a sad but stern voice the prosecutor confirmed that what he had told me was the truth as he had just spoken to my father. He even offered to call my dad if I did not believe him so he could confirm it. At that point, I knew he was telling the truth. His voice was soft and sincere. I could sense that he was having a tough time delivering such horrific news to me. He sounded apologetic and regretful.

I could barely hear him in the room; I was all alone and lost in my own world. I felt as if my heart had just been broken into thousands of pieces. The pain was too unbearable to be articulated. Something in me died right at that moment. I felt my entire body shut down. I was no longer able to speak or even cry. I was still in denial though I knew what I had heard was true. I still could not contemplate the idea of not being able to see my mom ever again. After all, my mom was very young and she had so much to live for. She had six children waiting for her at home and her precious 5-year old daughter was too attached to her. I could not get my baby sister out of my mind wondering how she was dealing with all that was happening. If I were home, I was sure she could find some comfort in my arms; but here I was locked away, far away from her.

I remembered the night of my arrest. I felt disgusted with myself for bringing all that on my family. I even blamed myself for my mom's death as I felt that the stress of that night must have caused her body to collapse. I wished I had been called in that first night to hear that I would be executed the next day – that news would have been easier to accept. My body was now noticeably shaking and the prosecutor knew that I could not walk back to my cell in that condition. While he knew I was over the initial shock, he wanted to give me a bit more time to pull myself together before sending me back to my cell. As he was leaving the office, he told me that it was okay for me to cry or scream as loud as I wanted and that I would not be punished for my outburst. He had put a Kleenex box in front of me in case I could not hold my tears any longer and I was glad he did. As soon as I heard the door close behind him, I started sobbing. I tried very hard to cry quietly but the pain was just too intense. I had lost control. It took so much strength not to cry in front of the prosecutor. Now that I was alone, I knew that I had to let it out. I was devastated. I was horrified. I felt I was chocking to death on my pain. Tears flooded uncontrollably. My face was all wet. Finally, I had no tears left and no voice. I became quiet. After several minutes of complete silence, the prosecutor, along with two of his guards, came in to escort me back to my cell.

The prosecutor requested, in a gentle voice, that I be quiet on the way back to my cell as he did not want other prisoners to hear me cry. I listened but could not respond. The guards were kinder to me on the way back. For the first time, they did not let me hit my head against the walls. They were quiet and walked slowly to ensure I would not fall.

Finally we got to my cell and the last thing I remember from that night was the sound of my own sobbing as soon as I saw my friends. They cried with me while they held me in their arms. It took me a while before I could give them the news. They were clearly distressed for me. After all, it was not too difficult for them to put themselves in my shoes and imagine how they would have reacted to such tragic news. I vaguely remember hearing one of the guards telling my friends that they were to do everything possible to keep me quiet. I am not sure how much it took for me to fall sleep that night but I do remember that my pillow was all wet in the morning. I woke up to the sound of the doors being unlocked by the guards so they could drop off breakfast trays. As I found myself in the cell again, I started crying. I guess I was still hoping that that was all just a dream, but now I knew it wasn't. I was now certain that last night was a reality that I had to live with for the rest of my life. There was no turning back now. The most horrifying thing I could ever imagine had happened.

A short time later I heard my name being called by the guards. They told me to get ready for another interrogation. I thought that I was being taken to get punished for disturbing the peace and quiet after I got to my cell last night. But at that point, I did not care about that or anything else. I cried all the way to his office. To my utter amazement, when I entered, I was treated with the utmost respect and kindness. I was greeted by the same prosecutor who had given me the bad news last night. I was ordered to take off my blindfold as he insisted on keeping his mask on. I thanked him hesitantly and took off my blindfold. He told me to let him know if there was anything else he could do for me to make me feel more comfortable during the time we were together. He said how sorry he was for all that happened and expressed his deepest sympathy. "Did you get any sleep last night?", he would ask. "Not really, I had nightmares all night long." "But I am glad I had my friends to support me.", I would respond. "Would you like something to drink; perhaps pop or fruit juice?", he would ask. "No, thank you, I am fine.", I would respond in a quiet voice.

Unfortunately I was unable to keep quiet and started to cry again. He could not handle seeing me in that state. He tried to distract me by reminding me that I was called in to be interrogated. "You know we beat up prisoners who make too much noise." "So you can consider yourself warned."; he said pausing briefly hoping that I would respond to him. "Well, you have got my blessing; go ahead and beat me!" "Remember though, you need a cable to do that; I don't see any here." "You might want to go out and grab one before you start threatening me.", I replied without crying. "Really, you don't see the cable behind you?" "Get up and look around to see that I am not bluffing."; he responded to me with conviction. Of course the gullible part of me believed his story. I got up and start looking for a cable everywhere. Soon I heard him laughing. I stopped and looked at him; only then I found out he was sending me on a wild-goose chase, so to speak. He reminded me of my younger brother who used to pull pranks on me al the time; and successfully I might add. He had chosen a nickname "Pinocchio" for me because I could be easily tricked and could not tell a lie or hide anything from anyone for any reason.

Perhaps in some ways, I reminded the prosecutor of his younger siblings; maybe a younger sister. That could explain his strange behaviour toward me. His focus was on diverting my attention and getting me to stop crying. He was smart enough to know what could potentially get me sidetracked, at least for a little while, and was getting me engaged on that. He talked about my political beliefs. He initiated a serious discussion on topics he knew too well I would react to. I wanted to be left alone so in the beginning I was still quietly crying and not responding to him, but he was determined to get me to stop crying so he kept demanding answers until I broke the silence. As soon as I would get all charged up and eager to take him on and prove him wrong, he would throw in a funny joke to change the subject and get me laughing. He imitated few funny characters on his staff, in such a way that I found it impossible not to laugh. He would then pick on the Mujahedeen leader, Massoud Rajavi who was a popular leader among all of their supporters at the time. "Don't you think his moustache needs trimming?" "Personally I don't find him attractive at all!" "He is short not at all charming so it must be pure luck that all his female supporters think he is hot!"; the prosecutor would say. I must admit, he knew which buttons to push to get me going. "Well I think he is much better looking than the ayatollahs that seem to be multiplying by the minute." "At least he shaves his beard and knows how to dress up!"; I would respond. I would make him laugh so loud that his staff could hear him clearly, though his office was far from their station. I was of course distracted too, so I was no longer crying. If I ever experienced mixed emotions simultaneously it was on that day. I was talking, crying and laughing at the same time and that was so out of character for me. I spent the entire morning with him that day and by the time I was back to my cell, lunch was being served. I went back feeling a bit lighter; but as soon as I saw my friends I started to cry again. It was as though they reminded me of the devastating news I had received a night before. I did not have much of an appetite but as my friends insisted, I ate a bit so they would not worry about me. Feeling exhausted, I asked if I could be excused to take a quick nap. As I closed my eyes trying to fall sleep, I thought about my mom, my baby sister and my family. I was not able to sleep properly but at least I had an excuse to lie down and cry quietly without bothering my friends too much. A few months before my capture, I had started taking sleeping pills on per my doctor's advice. I had difficulty handling all the stress in my life at the time; my mom's illness and the fact I could not go back to school were just a few things that were keeping me up at night. Now that things were a thousand times worse, I thought about asking for one sleeping pill per night. I spoke to my prosecutor the next day and he agreed to speak with the prison doctor about my request. The doctor approved my request immediately considering my unique situation, and I began taking sleeping pills again.

Every evening in the prison we all were able to listen in on special evening prayers on the radio. The radio was connected to loud speakers so everyone could hear no matter where in the building they were located. One evening as we were all listening in, I heard a prayer that I recognized well. It was my mom's favourite that she would listen to every evening. I remembered her crying every time. She asked God to give her a second chance so she could take care of her children a while longer. Listening in to that prayer just couple of nights after I found out my mom had passed away, brought back such painful memories that I lost control again. I was sobbing just like the first night I was informed of my mom's death. As I cried I became angrier. I was mad at God for not granting my mom's wish and for taking her away from us. I covered my ears so I would not hear that prayer. Before long, a guard came along to take me back to the interrogation room. I left with him crying non-stop on the way to the office. The guards were still kind to me and tried to comfort me in any way possible. As we were getting close to the office, I overheard my prosecutor talking to his staff. I could not believe what I heard him say. Perhaps that was one of the reasons I started to change my mind about him. I overheard him criticizing his people about the way they handled my case. He asked them to be extra cautious next time they arrest people my age. He suggested that the next time they were about to arrest someone, they better do their homework thoroughly to make sure tragedies like this never happen again. He went on to assure his staff that he had not changed his mind about capturing and punishing activists, only that he wanted to ensure those who were arrested really deserved it. He no longer wanted to see children in his prison. I now knew that I was the youngest prisoner in his prison. He sounded sincere and remorseful. He knew he was ultimately responsible for my arrest. That night he had ordered his staff to bring me in despite my plea to stay at my dying mom's bed for another couple of hours. He had only now recognized that someone like me should never have been arrested in the first place. And that the tip they received about my level of involvement had been inaccurate.

His guards sounded remorseful too, and vowed to be much more thorough in their investigation prior to making an arrest. My heart was pounding as I heard them, for the first time, admit to their mistake; but I thought to myself, too little, too late! At the same time, I hoped no one else would go through what I had gone through, at least in that prison. I knew they were many more prisons and depending on who was in charge, they each followed different sets of rules.

When we got close enough for them to notice us, they quickly ended their meeting. I entered the office and the guards left me alone with my prosecutor again. As always, he put on his mask and asked me to take off my blindfold. He asked how I was doing, what triggered me to lose control and cry that much. I explained that the prayer, which was just on the radio, was my mom's favourite. I went on to say that I could not handle listening to this prayer every evening because it was just making me too sad. As soon as I finished talking, he called to one of his guards and whispered something to him. The guard immediately left the office. When we were alone again, he promised that I would never hear that prayer as long as I was in his prison. He said that either the radio would be turned off during the regular time for that prayer, or that they would disconnect the speakers so the prisoners could not listen to it anymore. I thanked him sincerely and started to cry again. He could not handle seeing me cry. He started with his jokes again to keep me entertained and distracted. I was annoyed he was successful in redirecting my attention and getting me to laugh when I felt devastated. I wanted to go back to my cell so I could cry without anyone attempting to stop me, but he would not hear of it. We kept going for another couple of hours. I was getting restless. I bluntly asked him if he had nothing better to do than to entertain me. And he, somewhat jokingly, said that his job was to make sure that I did not cry. He said I was doing a good job prosecuting him but he was up for it so he challenged me to go on. He made me smile and soon he got me laughing again.

If I was ever surprised by his bizarre behaviour toward me before, he stunned me now. He told me that he was thinking of sending me home so I could attend my mom's funeral. Before I could respond, he went on to say that he would have a couple of his guards drive me to the cemetery and wait for me while I spent some time at her grave; and after couple of hours they would to take me back to prison. He suggested they would dress in regular clothes instead of uniforms, looking exactly like they did at the hospital when they arrested me. He assured me that they would leave their guns in the car so people around us would not feel uncomfortable. While I was surprised by his offer, he was more surprised by my reaction. Perhaps in his mind, that was an amazing offer, and anyone else would have accepted this with heartfelt gratitude, but I was furious at him for even thinking such thoughts, much less sharing them with me. I felt ridiculed and offended. Did he think that he knew what was best for me now, and what could help me with my healing process? Did he even for a second believe that I would take him up on his offer? As far as I was concerned, it was too little, too late now. I was the only one who could decide for me, at least in dealing with my personal tragedy. I remembered how much I pleaded with his men to let me stay with my mom that night, but they did not listen to me. Now that she was gone, they felt generous enough to consider allowing me to visit her grave?!

He was disappointed. After a while, he started to speak again, saying that there might be other ways for him to help me. He suggested that I could be released to go home for a few days to spend some time with my family. He assured me that his guards would only be watching the apartment from their cars, parked on the street across from our building, some sort of covert surveillance program. As an Iranian, he was aware of our cultural traditions when someone passed away. According to our tradition close and extended family members and friends would gather to grieve with the family of the person who had passed on. These ceremonies were designed to comfort those who had been left behind, and also to honour the memory of the person who had died. People would get together on the day of the burial; then on the 3rd day after the burial; also on the 7th day and then on the 40th day. As well, family members and friends would get together to visit the grave at the one year anniversary. The prosecutor knew that would enable me to attend at least one or two of those ceremonies. He was hoping this would help my family and me in dealing with our devastation.

He paused to hear my answer. Without any hesitation, I responded that I could not and would not accept this offer, either. Before he had a chance to come up with another, I started talking again. I told him how mortified I was to go home and face my family at this time; most certainly I did not think I could handle seeing my baby sister and my younger brother. I told him that I was exhausted and that I wanted to go back to my cell, if possible. I wanted to lie down. He was hesitant at first. He eventually agreed to let me go if I would give him one last chance to share yet another idea with me. I had no choice but to agree. He continued on to say that he could bring my baby sister to the prison to spend some time with me, with a guarantee of her safe return home. If I had said yes to this arrangement, my sister would be there with me tomorrow, and any day after that for regular visits for as long as my family and I wished. I was now in a state of shock but without hesitation I declined that offer as well. I did not have the strength or desire to share the reasoning behind my decision so I kept quiet after that.

I was convinced that my decision was for the best, at least under the circumstances. I felt that I had caused enough heartache for my family already; and I should just leave them alone to deal with this tragedy. I did not have the heart to put my baby sister through yet another painful experience. She had just learned that she would never get to see her mom again; and I did not think she could handle seeing me locked up too. I thought if I went back for few days and then had to leave her again, that could distress her even more.

When I finally spoke up again, I told the prosecutor that I felt dizzy and nauseated; could I please go back to my cell. He did not want to give up; but I insisted that I had heard all that I could handle for one day. He finally agreed to let me go, but promised that he would see me first thing the next morning to continue our discussions. As soon as I got back to my cell I started to cry. I shared with my friends what had happened. While they tried to be supportive, they looked disappointed to hear that I had not accepted one of those offers. In my heart though, I knew I had made the right decision. It was too early for me to come to terms with the harsh reality. Going home meant accepting the fact that my mom was really gone and I was not yet ready for that. At least in prison, I could go on living in a state of denial for a while longer, to tolerate the intolerable a bit better. Or perhaps I felt that I deserved to be punished more so it was best for me to stay where I was.

All that was happening around me was just too confusing. I knew that as far as the law was concerned, at least the new dictators' law, I was a criminal who deserved the worst. But now that I was in prison, one of their appointed officers was treating me as if I was his little sister. I wondered about that. Perhaps this tragedy had awaked the part of him that related to me as a human being, even a younger sister, and not a sworn enemy. I certainly started to look at him as a human being, whose biggest fault was to act according to his erroneous beliefs. With this new perspective, I slowly began to feel a bit more calm and peaceful. While I still blamed the new dictators for such tragedies and injustices in our country, I was less angry at those who were blindly following their orders.

Regardless of how I felt, my daily schedule, for the first couple of weeks after hearing about my mom's death, remained the same. Every morning and evening I would be taken to the prosecutor office to spend some time with him. He would spend a couple of hours, at each session, talking to me, making me laugh and making sure I did not cry while I was there. In almost all of those sessions, he would express how sorry he was that I was going through such pain. Finally in one of our sessions, he looked me in the eye and told me that he was willing to dismiss my case and drop all the charges so I could go home for good. First I thought I was not hearing him. I asked that he would repeat what he had just said. He did; and I heard him say that if I accepted his offer I could be released in no time!

I was speechless. I thought either he had gone completely mad or that he was just testing me to see how I would respond. Could it be that he had come to care for me in some way and truly wanted to help me out? Or could it be that perhaps he could no longer justify such violence and terror against innocent children? Nevertheless, I was unable to process all that was happening logically. After a while, I said no to his last offer as well. I told him that I would rather remain a prisoner for the rest of my life, or even to be executed, than to go home and face the world without my mom. And before he could say anymore, I told him, sarcastically of course, that I believed a dangerous criminal like me should be prosecuted and punished; this was best for our country. He was clearly upset and even more disappointed that I had turned down his last offer. But by then he knew me well enough to know I was stubborn. I had made up my mind. So he agreed to let it go and not to talk about anything like this in our sessions anymore. My decision made sense to me at the time. And if it was a wrong decision, it was because I allowed guilt, shame and rage to take control of me. I was now punishing myself for all the pain I felt I had caused my mom, my baby sister and the rest of my family.

As each day passed by, though I was going through the darkest moments of my life, my anger and resentment toward those who were responsible for my imprisonment subsided. And after the guards and the prosecutor involved in my arrest apologized and asked for forgiveness, I finally found the strength to truly forgive them. By letting go of my anger and hatred, toward those who had wronged me, I felt I set myself free. All of a sudden I felt more at peace; as if a heavy weight was lifted off my chest. Getting special treatment from the prison officials made my days in prison a bit more tolerable; nevertheless, I woke up almost everyday hoping that I would find myself at home, dreaming that my mom was calling my name, asking me to get out of bed and get ready for school. And then I would open my eyes to find myself in that cell; I would quietly start crying again.

Three weeks passed by; and finally during one of my routine visits to the prosecution office, I was informed that we were being transferred to one of the biggest and most feared prisons in Iran; Evin.

Evin was the place where they kept real criminals, drug dealers, murderers, and those awaiting execution for any reason. I could not imagine surviving in that horrifying place. I felt that my world had just collapsed before my eyes, yet again. I was being taken away from a place I had become comfortable in and from the people I knew and trusted. With all those thoughts running through my mind, of course, I felt anxious and apprehensive. Not knowing what was awaiting me, I begged the prosecutor to keep me in his prison for as long as he wished. He understood my fears but could not help me out with my last and only wish. He was clearly distressed to see me in that state. He explained that normally people would be held in his prison only temporarily. He and his team would prosecute the prisoners, look after preliminary paperwork, make the case and send everyone to Evin. There we would be put in front of a judge for sentencing. As he saw the tears in my eyes, he promised that he would do everything in his power to keep me safe. He said that he had put in a good word for me with a friend, another prosecutor in Evin. Though he tried to hide it, I sensed that he was worried about me.

CHAPTER 7 -
IN EVIN:

*"There's so much I had to say I know the words I left behind
And now I'm caught in a daydream with nowhere to run and hide
The world rushes by me, it's leaving me here all alone"
(Alanis Morisette Rain)*

****

That day finally arrived when we had to pack the few items we owned and leave Eshrat Abad Garrison. Though the rest of my cellmates were coming with me, I was frightened to leave what I knew. It was hard for me to say goodbye to the young prosecutor who had now become a source of protection for me. When he said goodbye, I sensed his apprehension. But, he put up a good front so not to make me feel more anxious.

With heavy hearts and much fear of what was waiting for us, we put on our blindfolds and soon were on our way to Evin. Once on the bus, we were reminded that we were not allowed to speak to each other or attempt to adjust our blindfolds in any way. There were a few armed guards sitting on the bus to keep an eye on us at all times. I was deep in thought, dreading what will be waiting for us. It must have taken a couple of hours before we finally arrived. We were led out of the bus and into a hallway. Once we got out, we were told our section guards would come and collect us soon to take us to our designated cells.

While the prolonged wait in the hallways of Evin was physically draining, I was emotionally exhausted and terrified of what was going to unfold before me. I had a pounding headache and felt a tremendous pressure in my temples and behind my eyes. The blindfold was too tightly tied, but I was afraid to adjust it. Then, I heard someone call my name, and before I had a chance to respond, my friends' names were called out, too. The four of us were taken to solitary confinement in Ward 209. We were told to line up behind one another, hold on to each other's "Chadors", and start moving. The guard grabbed the "Chador" of the first in line to get us moving down the hallway to our cell. Despite being blindfolded, we were at least able to see our feet. This was great, since it prevented us from accidentally stepping on each other.

On our way, the guard told us that we would share a solitary confinement cell while waiting for the general population to make room for us. The only image of solitary confinement in my mind was of the cell in Eshrat Abad. Though our old cell was too small for four people, we had no problem getting along. Thinking that the new cell would look pretty similar, I was not concerned about sharing yet another with my friends. In fact, I was happy that we would all be together again. After what seemed like a life time, the guard instructed us to stop. We then heard a door being unlocked and shortly after, we were locked up again. It was early afternoon when we finally got to our cell. Taking off our blindfolds, we glanced at our new cage. It was different from the one we were in at the previous prison. This looked more like a room in an attic; dark, damp and gloomy. The first thing we all noticed was a small toilet seat in the middle of the cell. In disbelief, I innocently asked my friends if they knew what that toilet was for. Letting out a nervous laughter, they confirmed my worst nightmare. We had to use the toilet in each other's presence! This cell was definitely built for one person, but now there were four of us there. I thought in this case they would make an exception and let us use a bathroom outside of our cell. I had a hard time imagining how we could bear such humiliation. Perhaps this was done on purpose to dehumanize us even more. I seriously considered not eating or drinking. Half jokingly, I told my friends what I was thinking, but immediately regretted it since I felt like a spoiled little girl who only thought of herself. Of course all of my friends were uncomfortable with such arrangement, but they were being mature about it. Sensing my embarrassment, my friends tried to comfort me by sharing their frustrations as well. We vented for quite a while before admitting to ourselves that we had to come to terms with this. We knew we had no control over what was happening to us, so we decided to come up with ideas that could help us bear such violation. Still apprehensive, we laid down, curled up and tried comforting one another. Suddenly we noticed written messages at the base of the walls, at eye level, apparently by those who were kept captive in our cell before us. A few prisoners had written their names and noted how long they had been held captive. Someone had signed his name and written below it, "Remember me". Most of the messages intended to keep our hopes alive. They were promising peace, freedom and an end to senseless killings and torture. They talked about light's victory over darkness though it appeared that the darkness had prevailed. It was disheartening to read those notes knowing that perhaps people who wrote them did not make it out alive. The thought of those who once occupied our cell being murdered turned our stomachs. Ward 209 had been reserved for prisoners who were going to be executed after being beaten into confessing their "crimes". But we were placed in that ward because of over crowding. Emotionally and physically exhausted, I closed my eyes and soon fell sleep.

I must have slept for about an hour or so before my friends' chuckles woke me up. They were examining ways in which we could make light of our awkward bathroom situation. We chatted a bit, mostly joking about the subject since all of us, thankfully, had a great sense of humour. We jokingly made predictions about who would go first. Then we talked about covering our ears, pinching our noses and holding on our breaths while someone was using the toilet. The person on the toilet seat faced the door; so we would sit facing the door. This way, the person would have some privacy! As well, we found some old newspapers there that we could use to cover ourselves while on the toilet seat. Last but not least, we promised not to laugh if the person using the toilet let out gas or if the smell was too awful. While our collective effort helped each one of us feel a bit less apprehensive, none of us yet had dared to use the toilet in the several hours after our arrival. Personally speaking, I was still horrified. But, soon we had no choice. I still feel sick to my stomach remembering what we went through. There were occasions when one of us had the sudden urge to use the bathroom while others were having breakfast, lunch or dinner; in which case the rest of us would stop eating. I could not think of anything more disgusting than to eat while a grown person was using the toilet two feet away. Not surprisingly, none of us had much of an appetite. Anyway the awful tasting food in Evin encouraged us not to want to eat much.

Our sleeping arrangement was yet another challenge. It was the matter of who would sleep next to the toilet seat at night. Our cell was just too small and someone had to sleep very close to the dirty and smelly seat. The only way was to take turns each night and wish each other good luck in dealing with that. Seeing how bad it was, I had a strange feeling that things were only going to get worse.

Unfortunately for all of us, I was right! Starting that first night, we could all hear the screams and cries of men and women being tortured viciously. This would normally happen somewhere between midnight and the early hours of the morning. The place that was being used to torture prisoners must have been close to our cell since we could tell with certainty if the person being beaten was a man or a woman. At times, after a long period of screaming and shouting, there was a period of complete silence. And after a while, we could hear them again; only this time, they only moaned and groaned. Perhaps they no longer had the strength to scream. When the guards were done with them, we could hear them being dragged through the hallways back to their cells. We did not get much sleep. It felt as if we were taking the beating along with those poor souls on that horrifying night. We covered our ears. We prayed. We cried. Yet, it went on!

As I quietly cried myself to sleep at night, I wondered if I would be able to endure such torture. I wondered if those poor souls could survive such torments; or would most of them die at the hands of their own countrymen.

On the second day, I was called to the prosecution office. The person who was waiting for me sounded very young. I had been forewarned by my cellmate who was questioned before me, that he was vicious and cruel. He constantly swore at her and found any excuse to hit her on the head during the interrogation. I was really nervous wondering how badly I would be treated. As he started talking, to my utter amazement, he sounded gentle. He asked very few questions. He was polite and considerate, giving me plenty of time to pull myself together and answer. His first question surprised me the most since he asked how I was feeling. I quickly responded I was okay. He mentioned that the chief of the old prison I was transferred from had given him enough information about my case. That was the reason he did not feel that I had to spend much time with him now. As long as I was in that ward, he would meet with me everyday to make sure I was doing well. Then he asked me if I had any questions for him. I asked how much longer I would be staying in Evin. He paused for a bit. Then he said that he could not make any promises about the duration of my stay, but confidently assured me that I would be fine in Evin. He went on to explain that after I was placed in the general population, I had to wait for my turn to see a judge for sentencing. After the ruling, if I was lucky enough to be found innocent, I would have to wait a bit longer for my paperwork to be processed before being released. He then gently asked if I could finish filling out some forms before he could ask his guards to take me back to my cell. It did not take too long for me to finish responding to questions which were pretty similar to the ones I had answered at the time of my arrest in the first prison.

As soon as I arrived, my cellmates circled around me to find out what happened. They seemed very happy to see my smiling face again; yet they were curious to find out about my session. Though I felt really tired, I gave them a quick briefing before taking a nap.

I got to visit that prosecutor two more times before getting transferred to the general population. The day finally arrived when we were notified of our transfer. We did not have much notice. I believe we had just finished eating our lunch when we heard someone pounding on our door. It was one of the guards telling us to take our stuff, put our blindfolds, on and get ready to move. In a few minutes, the door was unlocked and two guards led us out of our cell and into the hallway. We passed through metal doors connecting different hallways together. After about 30 minutes or so, we were told to stop and wait for the guards from the general population to collect us. We must have waited there for a couple of hours before they arrived. I had started to feel dizzy and nauseous. My blood pressure was always low and that was the reason I had a difficult time standing on my feet for a long period of time. We were not allowed to talk to each other, but we whispered to one another while holding hands. We were uncertain as to whether or not we would end up together, so we were saying our goodbyes in case we got separated. Finally, after what seemed to be lifetime, I heard my name being called out. I waited anxiously to see if the guard would call out my friend's names; he did not. I was being taken away and that was the last time I saw my friends ever again. It was devastating to be separated from the only people I had come to know and trust. I prayed that God would keep them away from any harm, and prayed that some day they would return home safe and sound.

I walked about fifteen minutes or so before I was told to stop. We were entering the women's general population so I had to wait to be received by female guards responsible for that section. In a few minutes, I arrived at the general population. As soon as I entered, I was asked to remove my blindfold; this was the first time I was able to get a quick glance at my surroundings. I nervously looked around to see if I can find a familiar face, but I knew no one. Feeling overwhelmed and lonely, I finally grasped the severity of the situation I was in. Seeing that many strange women who were going to be my cellmates was stirring up my anxious feelings. I spent five minutes in the office before being escorted downstairs to the room I was assigned to. When the guards confirmed that I could be taken to my room, they called upon a prisoner, the supervisor for my assigned room, "Moneer" to come by and collect me. She was to take me to my room, show me around and get me familiarized with my surroundings. The first thing that was brought to my attention was that the room I was going to be in housed 90 other prisoners.

The best way to describe the general population, where I spent the next three and half months, is to say that it looked like a very large duplex house. Full time prison guards had a couple of offices on the first floor; and the large rooms holding 90 to 100 people each, were in the basement. The rooms were located in a long, dark and very narrow hallway. Somewhere in the middle of that hallway, there was a bathroom with only two or three toilet seats and about three stalls with shower heads. The bathroom was old, dirty, dark and scary. It was big enough that I felt terrified to use it at night alone. And small enough to make me wonder how long we had to wait for our turn to use the bathroom or the shower. The rooms were almost as bad as the bathrooms. We did not have enough space to move around freely as there were too many of us. The air felt damp and there was an unpleasant odour in the room. Two small windows in each room, which were being protected by heavy metal bars, were the only source of natural light and fresh air for us. I remember how excited I would get when the sun was out. At times, I could hardly fight the urge to climb up those bars to feel the magical warmth of sun on my skin. When I looked out I could see the yard, where we could spend two hours each day to walk and get fresh air. Looking out, I could also see the building's flat roof with a couple of armed prison guards. Day and night, they took their rounds to keep a constant and close eye on the prisoners.

The sleeping arrangements were another traumatic experience for me, especially on the early days of my stay at the general population. We had to sleep on one side so that we could all fit in the room. The thought of being left alone with 90 strangers during the day was horrifying enough for me; now I had to accept sleeping with them at such close proximity. When we laid down, I could feel and hear the person lying next to me breathe. There was hardly any space between us. Since we had to sleep on our sides, if in the middle of the night we felt restless and wanted to get on the other side, we had to sit up and then slowly turn to other side. Considering that we did not have a mattress or even a thick blanket to sleep on, my back and my ribs were hurt and I had to change sides constantly before falling sleep. But that was the least of my worries; I was even more apprehensive about who would be sleeping next to me. I wondered what would happen if I had a nightmare and woke up crying in the middle of the night. I was afraid that my cellmates would get mad at me for waking them. Sleeping arrangement in Eshrat Abad, though difficult, was not as traumatic for me. First I only had to get used to three girls, who were very close to my age, sleeping next to me. Second, we could sleep on our backs, and turning to our sides was easier since we had a bit more space between us. Besides, I had come to know and trust those girls and felt safe with them.

Saddened by the harsh reality I had to face, I suddenly remembered how I used to call on my mom when I had a nightmare. It was not too long ago that I would find my way to my parents' bedroom seeking comfort. My dad would always agree to let me sleep in their bed. He knew I was too afraid to go back to my room. I remembered how I would fit myself in and find a tiny space on the bed while gently holding my mom or dad's hands. My dad gave in more easily. My mom believed that I needed to grow up and be more independent. He used to let me crawl into his arms and told me fascinating stories to help me fall sleep. The last thing before falling sleep was a gentle kiss on my forehead that made me feel safe. Now a couple of years older, I still woke up in the middle of the night after a nightmare, crying and calling out for my mom. As I closed my eyes in bed, I remembered the night that I was taken away from her. I remembered how she looked at me and I remembered her tearful eyes. My guilt, the anger and the disbelief kept me up most nights.

I cried every time I thought about my mom, my baby sister and my family. I cried myself to sleep while praying that God take my life so I could be with my mom. And I would wake up crying when I opened my eyes to find myself still alive and locked up in that horrifying prison.

My first day in general population was overwhelming. Quick glances at everyone in our room led me to believe that most of the people there were much older than me. There were people in their twenties; some in their thirties, forties, fifties and sixties. We even had few women in their seventies. I later on found out that those women were captured solely because they refused to lead the government agents to their children and grandchildren. No matter how much of a beating they took, they did not break down, they never revealed their loved ones whereabouts.

On that same day, I found out that I had to report to a specific team within my designated room. The prison officials had picked a few prisoners, the ones that they could trust the most, as the room supervisors. The responsibilities of the room supervisor included assigning daily chores to each team and keeping track of their daily, weekly and monthly schedules. In this way, a team that was responsible for cleaning the room for a week would not get the same responsibility for the following week, and so on. However, I was told later on that the unspoken responsibility of room supervisors was to keep a close eye on the prisoners and how their relationships with their fellow cellmates. Also, they were to listen in to prisoners' conversation where possible in the hope that some of them might reveal valuable information to be reported back to the prison officials. In return for spying on others, the room supervisors and a few other selected prisoners were promised shorter sentences and no more torture. I resented those people for what they did to others. People like "Moneer" made me uncomfortable. I could not be myself when I was with her. I feared I would get reported. I felt I was in danger and was afraid to be alone with her. Being around people I could not trust made me feel even more anxious.

The room I was assigned to consisted of 10 teams and each team had about 9 or 10 members. I finally was introduced to mine. I knew I would be eating, sleeping and working with them, so I hoped they were nice and friendly. They took over explaining how things worked around there and briefed me in on our daily schedules, chores and responsibilities. I found out what to do and not to do during certain times of the day and how to handle food distribution when it was our turn to help feed our room.

Thankfully, and almost immediately, I got to like all of them especially two women who seemed warm and compassionate. It seemed that each time I met someone new they turned out to be angels sent by God to look after me. First, it was the three girls I shared a cell with for almost a month. Then, it was the prosecutor and his staff who had a change of heart and helped me a great deal through the darkest moments of my life. Now, I crossed paths with two ladies, "Seema" and "Mehrnoosh" in my team who took a liking to me almost immediately. And later, they became a tremendous source of comfort for me for the remainder of my time, three months, in Evin. They were both about 8 to 10 years older than me and certainly the nicest people I had ever met. "Mehrnoosh" was single. She was the quiet type, an introvert. She was kind, gentle and caring yet she showed her emotions through her actions more than her words. "Seema" was married and had a one year old baby girl. I soon found out that her husband was also locked up in Evin. As I listened to her heartbreaking story, I felt guilty for feeling sorry for myself. "Seema" was arrested while she was out with her baby. She got to keep her baby for the first several weeks in Evin, but the prison officials finally arranged for her parents to take the baby home. Her pain was beyond my comprehension since I was not a mother yet. I could only imagine how devastated she must have been when she said goodbye to her baby. Her story was a sad reminder of what my mom went through the night I was taken away from her so violently.

As time went on and I got to hear other prisoners' terrifying stories, I wondered how they had found the strength to bear the unbearable.

As I was curious to find out what kept these people sane, I watched them carefully hoping to learn how they coped. Some found peace in comforting and supporting others; while others kept to themselves and appeared somewhat unapproachable and perhaps uncaring. Some felt closer to God and spent a great deal of their time praying and reading the Koran; and some looked as though they had turned their back on their beliefs and given up on God. There were those who shared what little they had to eat with others in need, and those who took from others when no one was watching. Witnessing such differing responses to seemingly same harsh reality was an eye opening experience for me.

My new found friends stayed close with me to make sure I was doing okay. "Seema" had now become my shadow. She sat close to me when we ate and at each meal she asked if I was still hungry. She knew that teenagers normally ate a lot so she was willing to give me some of her food to ensure I did not go to bed hungry. "Seema" slept next to me at night; and "Mehrnoosh" slept on the other side of me. I felt really comfortable to go to sleep surrounded by two people that I had come to like and trust. I had trouble sleeping. Every night "Seema" held my hands until I fell asleep. She also helped me with chores that I found a bit difficult to make sure my work would pass the inspection of our room supervisor. The chores included cleaning and dusting our room, cleaning the hallways, washing the bathrooms, washing the dishes after each meal, taking out the garbage, distributing the food among prisoners in our room, washing our own clothes, and looking after anything else that required our attention. Last but not least, "Seema" kept close contact with me at all times to warn me when I was being approached or questioned by prisoners who where there to spy on us. She was determined to keep me safe, and with each passing day I found myself more attached to her. Words cannot describe how wonderful she was and how much she cared for me. She was truly my guardian angle sent by God to keep me from any harm.

Gradually, I became more familiar with daily routines and got to know more people besides those in my team. I also found out that we could communicate with our families and how to write and send mail to them. Though our letters were censored, I believed our families looked forward to seeing our handwriting to at least know we were still alive. Also, we could provide them with a list of approved items they could bring to us in prison which was really helpful for all of us. Since we could have visitors once a month, most of us would ask for money, clothing, blankets, candies, nuts, and any other items that we needed. I remember my visits with my father and baby sister a couple of times during my stay. Visiting days were always saddening to me. It was heartbreaking to look at my baby sister's beautiful brown eyes and see how sad she looked. While I did not have the heart to discourage my father from visiting with me, deep down I hoped that he would not show up on scheduled visit days. I felt undeserving of my family's love and attention. I did not want my dad going through so much trouble to come for a visit each month. Seeing him was a painful reminder that my mother was no longer with us. There were other reasons I did not like visiting days. There were some prisoners who had no visitors; and there were others awaiting execution, not allowed to have visitors. Then, there were those who cried for weeks after the visiting days as they missed their families even more after each visit. Watching those people go through so much agony made me feel even more helpless and emotionally out of control.

However, the only way I could get the money I needed to buy much needed personal items from the prison shop was on visiting days. Though the shop was not located in our building, we had access to it through our room supervisor, "Moneer". All we had to do was to go through the list of available items, checkmark what we needed and provide her with the money, and she would handle the rest. On designated days, "Moneer" would purchase all the items, and upon her return, distribute them accordingly. Prison food was tasteless and was served to us in very small portions. As such most of us looked forward to getting some money so to purchase edible items, like cookies, dried fruits and nuts. There were times that I would go to bed hungry if I absolutely could not eat what they served for dinner. More often than I liked, we were served bread, butter and jam for dinner. I did not like butter or jam so I could only eat a small piece of plain bread, and went to bed on an empty stomach. It was on those nights especially I had trouble sleeping. At least I was making my team happy since they could divide my share of jam and butter among themselves. Breakfast was another challenge for me since I did not like what they served then, either - butter, jam or cheese, I only ate bread to keep me from starving until lunch time. For lunch, we mostly had tasteless and sometimes foul smelling mixed rice; and sometimes we had plain rice with chicken or some kind of beef stew. Rice was my favourite dish. Even though at times it looked and tasted disgusting, I still looked forward to eating it.

For our daily outdoor activity we had permission to go out in the yard for some fresh air and sunshine. However, due to a horrifying incident that took place at the yard later on, I no longer looked forward to going out. I spent most of my time in the hallway or the room. It happened one nice sunny day in summer. It was almost lunch time. We had just come inside after being in the yard for about an hour. We were quickly getting things ready before lunch was delivered. As each team took its place, on the floor, we noticed that "Mehrnoosh", my single friend, was missing. We called out her name a couple of times, but decided to start eating thinking that she must have gone to bathroom. I clearly remembered speaking with "Mehrnoosh" just before we came inside but I could not remember if she followed me in at that exact time. Our team sat close to one of the windows. As I started eating, I suddenly felt the urge to get up and look outside to see if "Mehrnoosh" was still out there for some reason. What I saw through that window will stay with me for the rest of my life.

"Mehrnoosh's" lifeless body was hanging from the metal bars of one of the windows across from our room. Her eyes were closed; her hands were hanging beside her lifelessly and her head was lolling. I could hear horrifying noises, what sounded like loud and scary snores, coming out of her. "Mehrnoosh" had hung herself using a scarf she had on that morning. I could tell that she had lost consciousness as she was not struggling. She looked dead! I must have been the first one to see her in the yard since we all knew that if the guards had noticed this they would have rushed to her rescue. Suicide is considered one of the greatest sins in Islam. Since prison officials claimed to be such devout Muslims they did their best not to let anyone take his/her own life while in prison. Ironically enough, killing people because of their political beliefs or religious affiliation was not considered a sin in their book!

Completely immobilized by terror, I was not able to find my voice to scream or cry. I was lightheaded and could hear my heart beating as if I had run miles without a stop. My knees were shaking and a cold sweat ran through my body. I climbed down the window, sat down and looked at my friends with my eyes wide open. As my mouth was extremely dry, I tried to reach for a glass of water, but my hands were shaking violently I could not hold the cup. I said nothing; only looked at the window and shook my head. I was clearly in shock. Perhaps I was too young to comprehend what I had just witnessed! As I looked at everyone in my team in complete silence, they suddenly noticed how pale I had become. Nervously, they asked if everything was okay; but I still could not speak. I finally came to and pointed to the window, but my silence felt like a lifetime. My friends quickly got up to look outside hoping to find out what I was trying to tell them. Suddenly, they began to scream. While they called for help, we heard emergency sirens going off. The guards rushed to the yard and hurriedly carried out her lifeless body. I remained glued to the floor. I was too traumatized to move.

I had no doubt that "Mehrnoosh" was dead, and each time I closed my eyes, I saw her hanging from the metal bars. I could not get that picture out of my head. The thought of losing one of the two people I needed most was unbearable. I followed "Seema" everywhere she went as I was too scared to stay alone even for a minute. It took me a couple of hours before I was able to cry out loud. When I had no more tears left I started to go over all of my interactions with "Mehrnoosh" earlier that day. Ever since she had woken up that day, she was not her usual sweet self. She seemed a bit distant and preoccupied, but since I sensed that she did not wish to talk about it I decided not to bother her. She was one of the very few people who always listened to me and gave me advice when I was down. But she was about 10 years older than me so, I felt that perhaps she would prefer to speak to someone with more experience. Suddenly, I remembered earlier that day, just as I was coming inside to get ready for lunch, "Mehrnoosh" had said goodbye to me. I innocently took her goodbye to mean "see you later", so I had jokingly said bye to her too. Now I understood.

She was clever enough to pick a time that almost everyone was distracted and busy with lunch distribution. Plus, the window she had picked to hang herself was located in an area that did not have great visibility from the flat roof where the guards were located.

Still in shock, I tried to make sense of what I had just witnessed. I remembered the story my friends told me about a girl who had hung herself in our bathroom several months prior to my transfer to general population. Apparently, early one morning a loud scream followed by a hysterical cry had woken up other prisoners. When people rushed to where the noise was coming from, they found the lifeless body of a girl. By the time the guards found their way in and got her out, almost everyone in that building had seen the dead body. Hearing that story had given me shivers at night, so much so that I was frightened to go to the bathroom alone.

Now that I had gone through the same experience, I could imagine how devastated my friends must have been to lose one of their cellmates in such a violent way. I wondered how they had survived and if I was strong enough to cope with what I had just witnessed? It was hard for me to fathom what had driven such a sweet, selfless and wonderful person like "Mehrnoosh" to want to take her own life! Someone that was loved by everyone and had so much love to give to others; and someone who still had so much life left in her! To take such desperate measures, one must truly be at the end of her rope; but was she? If she was, why did she not open up to her friends before she decided to end her life? I could not come up with any satisfactory answers.

"Mehrnoosh" was taken away. We did not hear anything until the next day when one of the room supervisors notified us that she was still alive. Apparently they got to her in time and had been able to resuscitate her. She was, of course, not in good condition, but doctors expected a full, yet long recovery. I had a difficult time believing that what I had heard was true. As far as I was concerned "Mehrnoosh" was dead. I saw, with my own eyes, how her lifeless body hung from the window bars in the yard. But when "Seema" confirmed that we'd have her back in a few days, I knew that was all true. Though I was extremely happy to hear such wonderful news, I was petrified to see her again.

"Seema" picked up on my fear and we talked about it at length. When she heard how I felt, she offered to get someone else in our team to sleep on my other side instead of "Mehrnoosh". I thanked her and promised to do my best to handle the situation in a way that I would not hurt "Mehrnoosh"'s feelings. I was embarrassed but I could not help feeling terrified. I was no longer comfortable having "Mehrnoosh" sleep next to me.

Several days later, we had our friend back. But I was not able to give her a hug or to welcome her back to our team. It was as though I was watching a classic horror movie where the dead person had just come back to life to haunt others.

To make matters worse, a deep and scary scar on "Mehrnoosh"'s neck, though covered with bandages, kept reminding me of what had happened only few days ago. It was heartbreaking to witness her struggle to talk, and how low her voice was if she wanted to say a few words. She was advised not to talk too much for the time being, but doctors had predicted that she would eventually get her voice back. She was clearly distressed and in a lot of pain. There was a profound sorrow in her eyes that made us all very sad too.

The first night of "Mehrnoosh"'s return was perhaps the most awkward time for all the prisoners, especially those who shared a room with her. Nevertheless, everyone empathized with her and tried to make her feel welcomed. "Seema" kept her promise and arranged for "Mehrnoosh" to sleep a little further from me. But I still had a tough time falling sleep because all that was too fresh for me. Each time "Mehrnoosh's" eyes met mine, I shivered. I held "Seema's" hands and cried myself to sleep. When I woke up the next morning and saw "Mehrnoosh" I felt ashamed of myself for behaving so immaturely toward her. Fortunately, she very understanding and did her best to make me feel comfortable around her slowly, but surely. With each passing day, "Mehrnoosh" looked and felt better. Her scary scar was healing and she was able to talk with more ease and comfort. And finally, one day I got to hear her story.

Apparently, the night before "Mehrnoosh" hung herself, she was called in to meet with her prosecutor. During the interrogation session, she had been given an ultimatum and was threatened with being tortured severely until she decided to cooperate with them. She had been beaten viciously so many times before; and the deep and scary scars at the bottom of her feet spoke of the severity of the beatings she took. Yet to date, they had not been able to break her down and get her to betray her fellow activists. Despite the vicious torture, she had found the courage and the strength to endure the unbearable pain yet remain silent. "Mehrnoosh" did not want to lead the agents to her fellow activists fearing that they would be executed right away. This time though, she admitted that she felt different. She was no longer sure if she had enough strength left in her to endure more torture. Fearing that she might betray her friends, she had decided to end her own life instead. At last, I was able to grasp the depth of her desperation and understand. While I empathized with her, as we all did, I must admit that I was angry at her too. I was angry not only because she almost killed herself, but also for putting all of us through such ordeal. Though I had always been compassionate toward others, at that moment I felt more selfish than empathetic. That troubled me. I could not deny how I truly felt, but I hoped that in time I would be more accepting of her. The more I got to know about "Mehrnoosh's" horrifying experience in prison, the more empathetic I felt towards her. I learned that she was among the prisoners who had gone through several surgeries as a result of severe and constant beatings. The guards were using thick and heavy cables to beat her up and she took most of the beating at the bottom of her feet. As a result of such serious injuries, prison doctors had no other option but to perform skin grafts. This procedure was designed to cover the non-healing wounds with skin removed from the healthy part of the body, normally hips or thighs. I later on found out that this method of treatment was effective in preventing infection. But it also served another purpose. It enabled the guards to continue beating up on prisoners' fresh wounds to get them to cooperate. Not too many people could remain silent through such excruciating pain. As such, confessions and giving out information leading to others' arrests were almost always achievable. I got goose bumps just by looking at "Mehrnoosh's' wounds and realized why she could not walk properly.

Now that I understood "Mehrnoosh's" situation better, I realized that her suicide, had it been successful, would have served two purposes: first, it would keep her friends safe for a while longer; and second, it would put an end to her agonizing physical and emotional pain. Later I discovered the third and perhaps most disturbing reason which pushed her over the edge. "Mehrnoosh" was afraid of being raped just before her execution. Since they had not been able to break her under many vicious torture sessions, she knew that she would be sentenced to death, execution by shooting. She was not married and according to what Iran's dictators claimed, executing virgins was considered a big sin in Islam. To deal with such technicalities that could potentially keep them from killing innocent women, they came up with a clever workaround. They decided to force the women on death row to marry guards or prison officials for one night. What they call temporary marriage, I call violating helpless women maliciously. According to the new regime, such sadistic acts were considered holy and aligned with what God wanted for his creations. I was disgusted to even think that anyone in their right mind would translate such an inhuman act, raping virgin female prisoners, into carrying out God's will. How could abusing a person in such a cruel way be considered a holy act?

Though I was now fully able to empathize with "Mehrnoosh", I thought of that incident as the biggest trauma I ever experienced during my stay in prison; perhaps after being told that my mom had passed away. However, there were many more reasons for my sleepless nights. Our building was located close to a hill which was used to execute prisoners. We called those mass murders. The common execution practice in Iran was to shoot prisoners down in groups and empty the last bullet in their heads in the end. Sometimes they were hanged but mostly they were shot down.

Due to our proximity, we could clearly hear the shots and that was extremely disturbing for us to say the least. I was told to count my blessings since not too long ago my friends were able to count the number of people who were executed as well. At first, I thought they were exaggerating until I heard the rest of the story. They explained that executions would normally start with mass shootings and in the end the guards would get close to each prisoner to fire the last shot (The Coup de gras) to ensure they were dead. So, to figure out how many people were killed on a given day, all my friends had to do was to count individual shots and they would have the correct number of people murdered. The executions normally happened at night time so on occasions, my friends would hear the shots as they were eating dinner. On those frightening nights, everyone would go to bed hungry. How could they eat while their fellow inmates were being gunned down?

Finally, due to frequent complaints by female prisoners, the guards had picked a place further away to carry out the executions. In this way, we could only hear the mass shootings but not the last individual shots.

There was something else that kept me up at night. I got to experience, first hand, that living under such extreme circumstances could bring out the worst in some people. At such young age that I learned that man's own survival comes first. I witnessed and heard of occasions where prisoners would steal each other's food, money and personal belongings. I got to see people who spied on their fellow inmates and caused them severe harm for a promise of reduced sentence. I was an idealist dreamer. Never in my wildest dreams could I imagine such betrayals. Perhaps when I was put in this situation I was able to understand and forgive such people for their actions. I learned that no human being was without a fault and not everyone can be altruistic under such severe circumstances. Perhaps when fear gets its ugly claws in people, love and compassion could not survive for long!

Another incident that stayed with me revealed, yet again, the fraud and manipulation in Iran's so called "justice system". One night as we had finished eating dinner, we were asked to gather in our rooms for a visit from a prison official regarding an important matter. We were notified that, in response to the United Nations' concerns after hearing rumours of torture and killing in Iran's prisons, our leaders had agreed to allow a select group of their representatives to visit Evin. We were cautioned to behave in a proper manner and to think carefully before we answered any questions. As well, we were warned of the ramifications if we chose not to follow these guidelines. In other words, we were to keep silent and not to share our horrific stories of torture and murder. Specifically, we were asked to keep quiet about the real reasons we were locked up. Iran's government officials knew that they could not justify their actions. We were reminded that while the UN team was going to be with us for about an hour or so, we would be spending a long time in Evin - another reason for us to not consider taking risks and opening up to the team. We knew none of those threats were empty and that prison officials fully intended to punish those who rebelled against them. So, we were both excited and nervous at the thought of the UN team visiting us; so much so that most of us had a hard time sleeping that night. When the UN team arrived, quite a few prisoners ignored those threats and spoke up. They showed their scars; shared the reasons why they were captured and held unjustly; and answered all questions truthfully. A couple of people in their 70s shared their heartbreaking stories which left the UN team speechless. Regardless of the attempt to keep us silent, the UN team got to hear most of our stories. As well, they got to see the ugly scars which spoke of the severity of the torture and beatings in Evin. The UN representatives looked astonished and disturbed. The translator accompanying the team was visibly shaken up. It took a lot of courage to speak up knowing full well that prison officials would retaliate.

And so they did. The very next day, those who had spoken up were called in to meet with their prosecutors; and almost all of them came back crying in severe physical pain from the beating they had received. The pay back process took about a week. That was one of the hardest weeks in Evin. For some of us, it meant physical torture, and for some of us, including me, it meant being a powerless witness to all that brutality and sadism.

About a month into my stay in Evin, I finally received notification of my court date. I was excited and nervous, but mostly relieved that I would get to know, once and for all, what they planned to do with me. I wanted to know how much longer I would stay in Evin. I also heard that I was quite lucky as many prisoners had to wait much longer before they were called in to court. Yet my apprehension increased as we got closer to the date. First, because I was afraid I would be sentenced to many years in Evin. And second, I had heard there was no guarantee that they would honour their own sentencing and would let us out at the appointed time. In fact, I knew of a few people who were told by the Judge they were to be freed but, for some reason, they were still in Evin for years waiting to be released. There was too much uncertainty. We were kept in suspense most of the time. Perhaps this was a strategy to increase our feeling of helplessness so we would break more easily. There was no justice system to appeal to, so no one could object to the brutalities that were taking place in Evin.

I was terrified of what the future held for me. Even if I did not get any sentence and was ordered to be released as time already served, I would not be considered innocent. No sentence only meant that they had not been able to find solid proof of my guilt as of yet. Consequently, prisoners with no sentence were under regular watch, even after their release, to ensure they would not be involved in any anti-government activities in the future.

My court date finally arrived. I was received by a male prison guard who was waiting for me outside of our building. I was led through long corridors before arriving at a small office I thought was a waiting area. I was told to take off my blindfold and that was when I saw three other prisoners, waiting for their turn in front of a judge. The image I had from a court was what I had seen in movies; and this office looked nothing like that. Soon after our arrival a young Ayatollah, a high ranking religious authority, arrived and sat behind a desk not too far from our chairs. He had a couple of armed guards standing next to him. In front of him there was an old duty desk. On that desk we could see some file folders we later found out contained our individual files. As soon as he sat down and glanced at everyone in the room, I noticed he was staring at me. I was not sure why he looked at me that way, but I felt really uncomfortable. It was as if he knew me from somewhere, but I knew I had never seen him before. I tried to look elsewhere hoping to redirect his attention. But anytime I looked up, I saw him staring. He seemed really young. Perhaps that was why I thought he could not be a mean person. He appeared calm and patient. Shortly after his arrival, he called out to us and we were asked to sit close to his desk so he could start our sessions. The office was small enough that we could hear what was being said to other prisoners going before the judge before us. Perhaps, we could not hear all of their conversations but we could clearly hear their verdict. Apparently, I was one of the lucky ones whose court date coincided with one of our religious celebrations. I had heard that the judges on those days felt a bit more generous and would go a bit easy on prisoners. On the other hand, I had heard that if a court date coincided with sad anniversaries, like a religious leader's death or an assassination attempt on one of the leaders, the prisoners would receive harsher sentences and would get treated rudely by the judges. In other words, with the exception of serious offenders, those who were arrested while carrying some sort of weapon, the fate of the rest of us pretty much depended on the judges good or bad moods. Considering all that, I was really glad my court day had coincided with one of our prophet's birthday. I could tell that our judge was in a great mood. As I waited patiently, the judge called out my name. I got up and took the seat close to his desk. He greeted me with a big smile and almost immediately asked me if we had met before. I quietly looked at him and quickly responded that I did not remember ever meeting him. He went on to say that this was the reason he was looking at me as soon as he entered the room. To end that conversation, I assured him that we have no one in our circle of friends or family who was an Ayatollah. The way I responded made him laugh. Quickly he collected his thoughts, opened my file folder, and pretended that he was reading it thoroughly. As I held my breath and prayed for mercy, he looked up again and asked me, half jokingly, how much time did I think I deserved for what I had done. I was not sure if I should take him seriously. I paused for a minute; then looked at him with a smile and said, "how about six months?" I could tell that my naïve and immature response worked in my favour. He smiled and said that I was free to go! He said that he felt I had done enough time to learn my lesson. He then wrote something in my file, looked at me one last time, and said that he had requested my immediate release. I tried not to scream and jump off my chair. Instead, I smiled genuinely, and said, "thank you." I was still in shock when I left the office. On my way back, I thought about the young prosecutor and how his efforts had kept me unharmed so far. Then I thought about the young judge and the way he had treated me. Though he was not mean to others in the room, he obviously treated me more favourably. I wondered why that was. When we got back to the general population, I shared with my friends, anxiously awaiting my return, that the judge had asked for my immediate release. They were extremely happy for me, but I could tell that they were also disappointed to hear that I would be leaving them soon. I, too, felt sad at the thought of leaving them behind, especially my best friends, "Seema" and "Mehrnoosh". I knew it would be as hard for them to see me go as it was for me to leave them behind. At least I could look forward to holding my baby sister in my arms once again and perhaps continue my schooling. But those I was leaving behind had nothing to look forward to.

It took about two months before I was called in to the prison office to be notified that I was being released. It felt as though I was just waking up from a four-month nightmare. I thought to myself that if all that had been real, why was I let out unharmed from a place where thousands of people got beaten up viciously, tortured sadistically and executed unjustly? I felt as though I lived inside a large bubble for four months, where I could not be harmed in anyway. Though the worst went before me, that bubble surely protected me. Could it be that I was kept alive to suffer further and be punished more later on?

I pondered those questions and much more, but it would be a very long time before I could truly comprehend all that happened to me.

Chapter 8 -
Unfolding events on the
Day of my Release from
Evin:

"I wanted a perfect ending; now I have learned, the hard way, that some poems don't rhyme; and some stories don't have a clear beginning, middle and end. Life is about not knowing, having to change, taking the moment and making the best of it without knowing what is going to happen next!!!" (Gilda Radner)

****

One morning as I finished my breakfast and got started on my morning routines, I heard my name on the intercom of the prison office. I was being summoned to report to the office. I anxiously looked at my friends for support. They assured me that they would be waiting for me in the hallway. I quickly walked up the stairs. When I got to the office, I was told that I had about fifteen minutes to pack my stuff and report back. When I asked where I was being taken, they said that I was being released. I was told that my father was waiting for me outside of Evin's doors. Feeling dazed and in total disbelief, I flew downstairs to pack my stuff and say goodbye to my friends. I almost shouted that I was being released - I was finally a free girl! I was too excited and unable to think clearly about what I wanted to take home with me. My friends were happy and sad to see me go, yet they offered to help me pack. Thanks to their help I quickly got ready.

I hugged and kissed all of them; held their hands and wished them much strength and patience. Saying goodbye to "Seema" and "Mehrnoosh" was harder that I thought. With tearful eyes I was finally able to say goodbye to them and promised not to ever forget their generosity and kindness. I then said goodbye to the other prisoners I knew and wished for them to be released from prison very soon. Some of my friends gave me their parents' phone numbers so I could call and let them know they were alive and well. I promised to get in touch with their families and said my final goodbyes. I hurried out of the room and flew up the stairs to report to the prison office. Just as I reached the office, I was stopped suddenly by our room supervisor who was believed to spy for the prison officials. She took me aside and looked me in the eye. I believe she was trying to intimidate me. She caught me by surprise, so I asked if there was anything she wished me to do for her upon my release. She collected her thoughts, calmly responding that she did not need anything from me. She continued on to say that she had me figured out. She knew that I was not a changed person in anyway. She warned me what would happen if I chose to disobey the new dictators' rules and go back to my old ways. She revealed that I would be the subject of ongoing surveillance by government officials until they were sure I had completely lost contact with the Mujahedeen or their supporters - a probation period that had no end. I tried not to dwell on what she said so I would not ruin my happy day. I shrugged my shoulders, assuring her that I had come to my senses, and that she would never see me there again. I said goodbye and wished her luck and rushed upstairs to the prison office.

Once there, I had a "short interview" also known as a mini interrogation session. I was asked numerous questions mostly about what I thought of our current government now, and how my new perspective would reflect my life outside of prison. As stubborn as I had always been in speaking my mind, I carefully answered each question trying to give them the impression that I was now a changed person. I confirmed that the Mujahedeen had no longer any influence on me, that I had learned my lesson and did not believe in their lies anymore.

Something powerful inside me took charge that day to help keep my true feelings and opinions to myself. To prove that I was no longer part of any anti-government group, I did what prison officials asked me to do. They wanted me to say that I was sorry for what I had said and done, though in my heart I knew I had not done anything wrong. They dictated what I had to say in front of a camcorder, mostly about how staying in Evin had been educational for me. As I was sharing my thoughts about Evin, and the fact that this place was not a prison but a school, I felt sick to my stomach. It was as though, with each word, I was stabbing myself in the heart. But something forced me to keep going. Taped sessions like this were collected to prove that Iran's leaders only had people's best interest at heart. They wanted to help people see the real truth and earn the right to go to heaven. What they called the real truth, I called their erroneous point of view, yet I kept quiet. My ten minute session was to show that people like me had converted of their own free will. The truth was, this was part of the conditions of my release. If I did not agree to it, I would have to go back to Evin! So I agreed to it hoping that they would buy my fake act. Fortunately for me, they did! I could not believe they were so easily fooled; but glad to finally hear that I was being released.

Finally, two guards came in to escort me out of Evin where my father was waiting for me. Just as I was being escorted to meet my father, I opened my eyes. I soon realized all that was just a dream. I woke up with teary eyes. That was probably one of the best dreams I had in a long time. As I got up, I let out a big sigh. I saw my friends getting ready for breakfast so I quickly shared my dreams with them and moved on to my daily chores. I had just started my tasks when I heard my name on the intercom. This time, I did not pay too much attention and carried on. Since I was still deep in thought, I assumed they had called on someone else to report to office. I heard my name again and this time my friends ran toward me to get me to respond to their call. Prison officials who had not yet seen me arrive, sent one of the room supervisors to find and bring me to the prison office. I was told to pack my stuff and get ready to go home and I had about fifteen minutes to report back to the office. I felt like pinching myself to make sure that this was not yet another dream. Nevertheless, I ran back to tell my friends that I was going home. Never in my wildest dreams could I have imagined that my dream from the night before could manifest into reality that quickly and that precisely. Was it sixth sense or clairvoyance? I never found the answer. But I was flabbergasted to experience such a mystery at such young age.

The people I had talked to in the prison office notifying me that I was being released; the office and the equipment that was used to tape my so called "I am sorry for my actions" speech; the corridors I had passed to get from one office to another; my interview just before I was led to my dad and all the other small and peculiar details were exactly as I had seen them in my dream. As I recalling my dream, I felt as though I was rewinding a movie that I had watched a night before. This time, I was the lead actor!

To this day, after nearly three decades, I still get goose bumps when I remember the events on the day of my release, and how they were an exact manifestation of my dream. It was as if on that night, for a brief moment, I was given the gift to see the future. How else I could explain having such an accurate dream. Since that time, on occasions, I had dreams that would turn into real events; yet that dream remained the most accurate and the most mysterious.

This was real! I was going home! I was apprehensive to go home knowing that my mom would not be there to greet me. That was one of the reasons why I refused the young prosecutor's offer to go home. I questioned my ability to face the reality that my mom was no longer with us. While I was in prison, I still kept hope that all this had just been a nightmare that I would one day wake up from. A million thoughts were racing through my mind making me wonder if I could find the strength to deal with such emotional turmoil. I wondered how my family would receive me; and what they would think of me! I thought they would blame me for all the tragic events in our lives since the night of my arrest. I was not sure if I was strong enough to look my baby sister and younger brother in the eye without crying. All of a sudden, the thought of going home brought up all the pain and uncertainty I had tried for months to bury deep inside me. It was like going back in time reliving all the pain I went through, starting from the night of my arrest. Nevertheless, I did my best to pull myself together and tried to change my focus as much as possible. I tried to think of my younger sister and how happy she would be to see me back at home. I knew I had to find a way to manage my emotions; so I tried to envision my dream, and to picture myself at the university.

Buried deep in thoughts I waited for my release papers to get processed. Each minute felt like a lifetime. My knees were shaking; I felt nauseous and out of breath wondering what was waiting for me when I leave Evin. After a couple of hours, all the administrative items were out of the way. They were finally ready to take me to my father who waited for me outside of the front gate. Feeling chocked up with so many mixed emotions, I swallowed my tears and followed the guards to front gate. Radiant beams of sunlight almost blinded me as I was led out. With my eyes half closed, I saw a frail, white-haired, anxious looking old man rushing toward me with open arms! My heart sank as I realized that was my father. He looked as though he had aged decades during the past four months. Still in disbelief, I gave him a hug; he kissed me on the cheeks, and within minutes we were in a cab and on our way home. I don't remember talking much on the way. Perhaps I was afraid to cry as soon as I opened my mouth so I chose to remain quiet. I was still in awe over the events that had transpired just before my release, so I felt dazed and confused. As the cab moved along, I stared at the streets and people and wondered if I belonged to that foreign world anymore. Nothing seemed familiar to me as though I had been away for decades. I was mourning over the loss of those I had left behind in prison; those I had come to love and care for deeply; and those who supported me through the most difficult times of my life. Yet again, I felt as though I was stepping into an absolute unknown, and the road ahead seemed deserted and lonely.

Chapter 9 -
Life after my release
from Prison:

"We can easily forgive a child who is afraid of the dark. The real tragedy of life is when an adult is afraid of the light." (Unknown Author)

****

As we got closer to home the intense fear that was growing inside of me grew stronger. I felt overwhelmed and very much alone. I knew my family would not realize the depth and severity of the scars I was carrying inside. I chose to keep everything in.

I had spent four months in prison, yet it felt like an eternity. Our home no longer felt like my home to me. Nothing looked, smelled, felt or sounded familiar to me. It was as though I had never lived there before. Fear and guilt overwhelmed me. I felt estranged from those I loved. It was as though I was carrying a deadly virus inside; and to protect my loved ones, I wanted to stay as far away as possible. From my vantage point, those I once knew and loved no longer loved me. I even questioned if they were happy to see me alive, despite how kindly they behaved toward me. Such self-defeating thoughts made the heavy burden I carried on my shoulders feel much heavier.

Once at home I was greeted by my brothers and sisters. As happy as I was to see them, I was heartbroken to set foot in our home knowing that my mom was no longer there. I quickly went to my room to get changed into something more comfortable. As I was getting ready to sit down and enjoy a cool glass of water, I was hit with yet another bad news. My father informed me that he was planning to remarry as soon as possible. It was as if someone had hit me over the head with a baseball bat. The whole world collapsed before my eyes. I felt nauseous. I was lost for words. The thought of someone else replacing my mom was just too devastating to contemplate. I still had a hard time believing that my mom was gone. How could I accept that she was being replaced that quickly? Would this mean that I was losing my father too? After all, I had heard many horror stories about how step-mothers treated their step-children and how widowed fathers allowed all that to happen. I was shocked that my father could think of another woman while it was only four months after my mom's death. I was angry and resentful. But mostly I felt helpless as I knew we could not challenge my father's decision to remarry. I sank down on a sofa in our living room so I wouldn't fall down, and drank a bit of water. My mouth felt really dry. Unable to speak, I found myself staring at the empty space in the living room where my mom's bed used to be and drifted away to what seemed like another lifetime. I remembered when my mom was still alive. My memories were still too fresh. I could clearly see her shrunken body on that bed. I remembered her when she prayed and tearfully talked to God. I heard her when she was asking for a miraculous healing from her deadly disease. I recalled how much pain she was in as she begged God for more time with her children. I could see her pale face and her big beautiful brown eyes filled with disappointment and distress. She looked frail and exhausted. It was as though she did not have much life left in her. She trembled each time she laid eyes on her baby girl and tried to hide her bruised body from all of her children. The deep bruising and bumps all over her body were the result of chemotherapy and many other medical procedures performed on her. Cancer had now spread to her lungs so she coughed constantly, and was short of breath most of the time. She could not sleep lying down so we had put a few pillows to lean her elbows on and that was how she slept, while sitting on her bed. Most nights she was only able to rest her eyes as the excruciating pain kept her up all night long. As a result of her sleeping arrangements, she had large bruises on both her elbows and on her hips.

She was pretty much all bones anyway. Putting pressure on those areas was more painful that anyone could ever imagine. No amount of heavy pain killers, no matter how strong, could alleviate such pain.

As my eyes were filled with tears thinking about my mom, I was brought back to the present time when I heard my father calling out to me. Apparently, he had gone on talking to me about his reasons for remarrying. My siblings had clearly voiced their objection so he was hoping that talking to me alone would help get me on his side. And when he had not heard any response from me, he had called my name to bring me back to reality once again. I felt no empathy toward him. In my eyes, he was only thinking of himself. I remained quiet and did not to respond to him, and said very little to anyone else for the remainder of the day. To cry in peace and quiet, I locked myself in the bathroom throughout the day, until it was time to go to bed, when I knew I could cry without attracting attention.

From the next day, our house was busy again. Our neighbours and family members visited to welcome me home. I did not look forward to those visits since I put myself under additional pressure not to cry in front of them. Hiding what was eating away at me was not easy as I had always been transparent. People could see through me and beyond my polite but forged smile. I only spoke when I was spoken to and kept my answers short and vague. I knew they cared for me, and wanted to help out as much as possible. But I was in no shape to share with them my most intimate thoughts and feelings. The only thing I did communicate eventually was the fact that I was in no way harmed physically; unlike most other prisoners. Among our neighbours, I was closest with an amazing lady who was always there for me. I appreciated her in my life so much and never took her kindness and generosity for granted. Her name was Pari and she was yet another earth angel God had sent to watch over me.

After a few weeks I decided to find out how I could finish my studies and obtain my high school diploma. Of one thing I was certain, that as someone with a prison record, I could never enter any high school. My father, through a family member who was working for the board of education in Tehran, helped me find dates and times of final exams for grade 12. I knew I had to get my hands on some used books and study at home to get ready for the exams. I had the option to just take the tests at the board of education which suited me at that point.

Fortunately, despite the entire trauma in my life, I was able to successfully complete the requirements and pass all of my exams; and so I obtained my high school diploma. I was thrilled at my accomplishment and had a glimpse of hope that I would be allowed to enter the university as well. I thought, perhaps unlike what I was told in Evin, I could get lucky and no one would run a background check on me. If I happened to pass the entry exam, which was as difficult as writing the MCAT (Medical College Admission Test), they might go easy on me and allow me to continue my education in university. In those days, it was not enough to pass the entry exam for universities. We also had to pass the background check to ensure we had no criminal records. Anxiously hoping for a miracle, I enrolled in the first round of exams and took the test. Successful applicants' names would get published in one of our local newspapers. I clearly remember the day when my family and I anxiously looked through the entire newspaper to find my name. To everyone's amazement, including myself, I did pass the test and was qualified to write the second test that would ensure my entry to university. Now I was even more motivated. I showed up for my last written test with enthusiasm and much confidence. The second test was a whole lot easier for me and I had full confidence that I would get admitted to any university I chose. Perhaps I was still in denial about one important determining factor, and that was the background check. Just before they published the results for the second test I found out, through our neighbours, that government agents were conducting a background check on me. Pretty soon my long lost dream shattered before my eyes when they pulled out my prison record and found out that I had just recently been released. And so my admission was turned down. Perhaps if I did not pass those exams I would have handled things a lot better. But knowing that I was among a few selected people who actually did pass but was not allowed admission was a hard pill to swallow. As hard as I have tried to forget that day, almost three decades later, I can still remember how I felt when I found out for sure that I could not continue my education. To say that I was broken hearted is understatement. After my mom's death, that was the most painful burden I had to carry on my already fragile shoulders. Another part of

me died on that day. I mourned this unjust death for years to come.
Many times I wondered if life had been easier had I stayed in Evin.
I wondered if I could ever be happy again. And as difficult as it is to
admit, I wished that I had been killed in Evin.

MY FIRST JOB AS AN
ADMINISTRATIVE
ASSISTANT:

"Do not pray for easy lives. Pray to be stronger people!
Do not pray for tasks equal to your powers.
Pray for power equal to your tasks."
(Phillips Brooks)

****

It took me a while before I was able to force myself to accept my fate.
I thought about getting a job so at least I would get out of home and
get busy doing something. After much thought, and with the advice of
a friend, I enrolled in a typing class to see if I could find a clerical job
somewhere to keep my mind off my miseries. My dad had remarried by
that time; exactly a year after my mom had passed away. Staying at home
did not seem like a good idea. In addition, I was not able to contact my
friends very often, fearing that I might jeopardize their safety. Ever since
my release from Evin, I had noticed an unmarked car following me each
time I left he house. As much as I needed my friends during the most
difficult times of my life, I knew I had to stay away. I felt betrayed by
the universe in so many ways. First, it took my mom away from us in
such a violent way. Then it threw me into prison to spend four months
of my life in horror and dismay. If that was not enough, it replaced my
mom with a strange woman none of us could connect with in any way.
And last but not least, it took away my lifelong dream of becoming a
university professor and all my hopes for being happy. The grand finale
was the painful separation from my best friends, those I had known for

years before the time of my arrest and those that had become my best friends in prison, whom I needed the most.

I knew that we, as human beings, only live once, but now I had come to believe that we could die quite a few times while we were still alive. At least that was how I felt at that time. Entering university was more than a dream for me. It was a bridge that was supposed to take me from where I was to where I wanted to be, where I felt belonged. When that bridge got blown away for no good reason, at least in my eyes, I felt as though I had lost everything. I was afraid to close my eyes and go to sleep. I was haunted by a horrifying nightmare each time I fell asleep. In my nightmare I saw that I got separated from the rest of my family. Thankfully, they were alive and well but they were kept so far away from me. I was able to watch them from a distance with tearful eyes; but no matter how much I called out to them they could not hear me. It was as if they had not even noticed my absence as they seemed to go about their lives merrily. My nightmares were the reflection of my traumatic rejection from all the universities in Iran. The universities were still open and accepting of thousands of people, only I was prohibited to go through. It seemed as if the universe was plotting against me. One of the biggest universities in Tehran, the one I was planning to attend, was only a few minutes away from our house. Day in and day out, I got to watch young people entering and exiting through those gates. My heart sank every time I watched them. I cried quietly as I prayed for a miracle.

What would I do with my life now, I asked myself. I never had a chance to come up with plan B. I could not find anything more fulfilling and blissful than what I already had chosen for myself. I never thought about planning my wedding or a white fenced home and children. Ever since I was a little girl, I daydreamed about getting my doctorate. I envisioned myself as a university professor living her passion, teaching, learning and being of service to others. In all of my make believe games with my friends, I was the teacher. Instead of playing with dolls, I had a small blackboard and many colourful pieces of chalks for a teacher/student pretend games. When I started school, I always volunteered to help out those who had difficulty with a particular subject. And as I grew up and entered middle school and later high school, I tutored other students during our breaks, and after school, and on weekends.

I believed, intuitively, that everyone had the potential to learn and do well. I discovered that people had different learning styles as each person has special talents and aptitudes. Some people were stronger in specific areas and not so strong in others. But the "not so strong part" in people did not mean that they could not learn that skill. It only meant that they had to go about learning it differently; or perhaps work harder at it. Though all through my school years I was always an honour student, I never thought I was smarter than the rest of my classmates. Perhaps this was one of the reasons why they felt comfortable with me, and the reason I had quite a few students asking for my support.

Considering the importance of school in my life, I had a hard time dealing with such a harsh reality. Could this have been just a nightmare that I would wake up from soon or was all that real? If that was all real, why was I the chosen victim? Was I that awful to deserve such a fate? Was I deserving of such torturer? The more I pondered on those questions the more frightened and depressed I became. And since I could not find answers to my questions, I made up stories about how bad I was and how I got what I deserved. I even blamed myself more than I blamed the regime for all the suffering I had put myself and my family through. Life had lost its purpose and meaning for me. I felt no true desire to go on. I could not imagine opening up to my family and friends to share my pain. I felt that I had done enough damage already, especially to my family, that I could not allow myself to fall apart and take them down with me. I shut down and buried what was eating away at me from everyone, especially those closest to me.

Somehow I managed to complete my typing training. While I still had no idea what I was able to do, I reached out to people around me to help me find a job. By chance, I got connected to one of my high school teachers, I knew for sure was not a government spy. When she heard about my dilemma, she offered to speak to her husband, a successful businessman, to see if he could help me in any way. I gladly accepted her offer. Her husband was more than willing to help out. As it turned out, he knew quite a few senior executives who were running medium to large size companies, some of whom were his friends. He was able to get me connected with an executive who was looking for an administrative assistant immediately. My teacher's husband confirmed that the company was willing to provide training now that I had typing skills, especially since I came highly recommended. So, thanks to my teacher's husband, I was hired into a semi-private company with a great salary to assist the CEO and two other senior executives. As grateful as I was for this lucky break, I was stressed out and anxious for several reasons. First, I wondered if people could see through me and find out that I really did not like what I was hired to do. As well, I felt I was betraying myself by giving up on my dreams and settling for a whole lot less than I wanted to do with my life. I was really concerned about whether or not I could live up to my managers' expectations, and provide them with the type of support they needed. And last, but not least, I did not want to let my teacher and her husband down. I felt that for all they had done for me, the least I could do was not damage their reputation or make them look like fools in front of their peers. After all, it was their recommendation that got me the job in the first place.

Despite all the self-defeating thoughts, I was able to pull myself together and start my very first job at the age of 18. For the first couple of months, I cried at work every day. On a daily basis, during our lunch time, I would go into an empty office that belonged to one of my managers, close the door and cry for half an hour or more. Then I would say my prayers and ask for strength to keep going. And when I had no more tears left for that day, I would go to the bathroom, wash my face and put on a big smile before everyone got back from lunch. And each night just before I fell sleep, I cried, and prayed that I would die in my sleep.

And that was how I got ready for the next day in the office. I got up very early the next morning to get to the office so I could catch up with all that I had to do and to get a head start before my managers arrived. Not only would I start earlier than I was supposed to, I also left way after my working hours were done. My goal was to ensure that all my deliverables were taken care of on time, since I felt my lack of expertise and experience could potentially cause some delays. But in reality it was that I was never given proper training, so I had to figure out most things on my own. The lady who was supposedly in charge of my training, whose position I was taking over, wanted to prove to management that no one could replace her. She had been promoted, and by no means, did she want her job back. But she did not want to make things easy for me either. I was too innocent to understand her unpleasant and uncooperative behaviour. But I was not ready to give up and call it quits just yet. In fact, I was willing to go to any length to ensure I was not letting anyone down. I felt that I had done quite a bit of damage already, especially to my family, and that I had no right to fall apart. I knew no other way but to be my warm, friendly and respectful self, and ask for support from anyone else who was willing to help out. At 18, I was the youngest employee in our office and probably the most enthusiastic and hard working person in that company. I always had a big smile when I greeted people and soon my colleagues warmed up to me and enjoyed having me around. They admired my determination and commitment to learn and so they were more than willing to teach me all that I needed to learn. I must have had a much smaller ego at that time, since despite that lady's unkind manners, I still treated her with utmost respect. Pretty soon she became a friend as well, since she could not find a reason to dislike me. To everyone's amazement, including my boss and the executive management team, I learned everything there was to learn in about a month. But that was no surprise to me. I was always a quick learner and had a genuine passion for learning. I had an amazing memory so I never had to ask the same question twice. Before long I was the talk of the office and I constantly heard compliments about a wonderful job I was doing. In about three months, not only had I learned how to do my job efficiently, and actually implemented new processes for the administrative department, I also learned how to backfill for our sales department, deal with clients onsite and even backfill for the accounting department. The funny thing was that I had always labelled myself as someone who was not good in math, and I truly never showed any interest in becoming more familiar with mathematics, either. However, I felt motivated to learn enough about accounting so I could backfill for someone who was sick or on vacation in that department. My motto was there was nothing in that company I could not learn about or help with. My boss was so confident in me that he was now taking me on inspection trips to our out of town factories. He wanted to give me a chance to help with implementing effective safety procedures so to create a safer environment for our factory workers. As such I became even more motivated to keep going and learn as much as possible.

I will never forget my first trip to one of our factories. I almost caused serious injury to one of the young factory workers. I remember him clearly; he was working with dangerous looking equipment cutting through thick metal. He needed to pay undivided attention to what he was doing. As soon as he saw me walking around the premises, he forgot what he was doing and just stared at me. As a result, he almost burnt himself, but thankfully he responded quickly and shut down the power on time. He looked embarrassed as he noticed that my boss and I had just witnessed what happened to him. While I found all that funny, I was relieved that he came to, just in time, and a serious injury was prevented. In a way, I thought my presence had defeated the real purpose of my visit. I was there to help my boss create a safer environment and I almost caused pandemonium myself! However, I understood that factory workers were not used to seeing a young girl at the site. But I could tell that they were pleasantly surprised since they were more than willing to spend time with me to answer my questions. That worked to my advantage. I was able to provide my boss with valuable input to help him with his preliminary findings. I enjoyed my first trip as I found it educational for me and memorable for the factory workers whom I visited that day.

In a strange way life had started to look a bit more pleasant to me. It seemed as though I had found another purpose in life and new ways in which I was able to make a contribution. Yet as days turned into weeks and weeks into months, I started to feel bored. I was ready to move on since I felt I was putting my heart into something that was not satisfying to me. I could not picture myself doing the same thing for the rest of my life. Some of my colleagues sensed my restlessness and they joked about it. They suggested that I would become one of them pretty soon and behaving the way they did: coming late; leaving early if they could get away with it; doing just enough not to get fired, showing no interest in learning new things and meanwhile, counting the days to their retirement. After all, the only thing that kept most of them going was the pay check at the end of the month; so they could not understand the reason behind my restlessness. It was true that I was not passionate about what I was doing, but I felt differently about things than my colleagues did. I wanted to do my very best with what was entrusted to me. I took pride in knowing that I have been able to contribute to a success of our company, but I felt like moving on to new ventures.

My teacher was getting excellent news of how I thrived at work through her husband and she was proud of me. Most times when I was at her house to report my progress and to catch up with her, her sister, who had become a good friend of mine, was there too. She and I were closer in age; both single and both had similar interests. We soon became best friends. My teacher's sister was also working in a company which was only few blocks from where I worked. Since she normally finished, about half an hour later than I did, most days after I finished work I would walk to her office to go out for dinner or to the movies afterwards. We had so much in common, truly enjoyed each other's company, so the frequency of our outings increased. During my regular visits, I got to meet many of her colleagues. I also met the president of the company who was also close friends with my teacher's husband. He had heard about me through him. In fact, that was the company to which I was sent to take my typing test as part of the hiring process. I remember how badly I did on my test. I was trained on a manual typewriter and they used an electronic one, so I failed my test. They sent my typing test results to the company that had agreed to hire me. But since I had come highly recommended, they agreed to hire me anyway.

During one of my visits while I was waiting for my friend, the president of the company approached me to ask if I could spend 15 minutes with him. I wondered what that was all about, but agreed to meet him in his office. He went right to the point and asked if I was willing to consider leaving my company to join his. I was caught by surprise. Before I could answer, he went on to say that I would get a promotion and a substantial pay increase if I decide to accept his proposal. I was flattered to hear his generous offer, but I was not even tempted to think about leaving my own company. More money, better title or even being closer to my best friend did not measure up to what I was getting at my own company. My boss and his peers had given me the opportunity to learn and grow when no one else was willing to hire such an inexperienced person. They were patient with me while I was learning and always treated me with utmost respect. My contributions were always acknowledged and I felt an important part of the team.

My boss was positive and enthusiastic and he kept an eye on me as though he was looking out for his younger sister. So my answer to the president was a resounding no. He did not give up and tried to find a way to convince me; however, I stopped him and confirmed that I would not be changing my mind about this. Instead, I offered to take the lead and team up with the employee I was supposed to replace, to create and implement a more efficient and user friendly administrative system. The president was speechless; and since he was smart enough to know that I would not change my mind about his offer, he gratefully accepted mine. He asked how soon I could start as he could not wait for this project to get started. Our arrangement was for me to be there everyday after work and work about an hour or two depending on my availability. Apparently my counteroffer made so many people happy. First and foremost, my boss who was now certain he would not lose me. My boss was friends with the president who had offered me the job so when they spoke the next day he had found out about my refusal to leave him and his company. My boss called me in for a meeting the next day. During the meeting he told me how impressed he was when he had heard the story and he thanked me for choosing to stay with him. He also promised to get me more involved in all that was happening in our company so that I would not feel bored. Next it was the man who would have been demoted had I agreed to take over that position; so he became one of my good friends when he found out that I had turned his boss down. The president of this company was happy since he now had the extra help without having to pay for my services. And last but not least my best friend was very happy to have me there after hours since that made it easier for us to go out afterwards. And I must admit I was really pleased to know that my decision affected so many people positively. It was true that I had said no to a potentially better career opportunity, but my gut feeling was telling me that I had made the right choice and I never regretted my decision afterwards.

I got started on my second job; it was amazing to see how much energy I had left in me after a full day of work. The only time I considered, "my break time between the two jobs", was the walk between the two offices, mine and my friend's. After I was done for an hour or two working in that office, I still had enough energy to go out with my friend. The busier I became the less time I had to focus on my misery. As a matter of fact, I had become less depressed and much more enthusiastic about everything. As I started to enjoy my new life, a few months into my volunteer work in that company, I met a man whom, in about 18 months, would become my husband.

CHAPTER 10 -
ENGAGED TO BE MARRIED
AT 19:

"The greatest healing therapy is friendship and love." (Hubert H. Humphrey)

****

In Iran, especially in those days, women got married at a young age. When I was in school almost all the girls in our class talked about was how anxious they were to get married and have a family of their own. I felt like an outsider. I never contemplated getting married at such a young age. My vision was to spend an additional six to eight years at university after graduation. I always envisioned marrying someone who, like me, loved school, teaching and learning but I thought that would happen in and around my early 30s. But apparently life had something else in store for me. I heard a quote once I believe the author is John Lennon, that truly resonated with me. It said: "life is what happens to you while you are busy making other plans." And I found that to be very true in my case.

My life took another detour when I met this man. As we started seeing each other outside of work I began to appreciate his company. I could tell that he liked me a lot so I agreed to give this a chance and see where life would take us. As is true in most new relationships, the process of getting to know someone new was quite exciting. And it is also very true that in the beginning we consciously, or unconsciously, ignore some red flags so not to spoil our new found fascination. While I behaved like most other young people who thought they are in love, I was just too naive to determine if he was the right match for me. I knew nothing about his family, his vision and goals, his perspective, his life experiences, his likes and dislikes, and in general all that makes a man in my eyes. The only thing I knew about him was his age, he was 7 years older than me, and what he did for living. He was handsome and genuine. Most definitely I was still too young to know myself well enough to choose a great match for me. I just knew that I was attracted to him and constantly ignored my gut feeling about the whole situation. I could tell he was as a nice person with a good sense of humour who was also attracted to me. He was generous and spontaneous. Later on, when I found out that he actively supported another opposition party that fought against the regime; now I liked him even more. Though the opposition party he belonged to was at odds with the party I supported, I still found him courageous to take a stand for what he believed.

One day at the office, he invited my best friend and me to attend a trade show with him. He was representing his company and was responsible for setting up the booth and promoting their products. I was excited to attend, especially since he offered to drive us to and from the exhibition place as it was a great distance away from where I lived. We had fun at the show and enjoyed visiting and getting information about other companies. On our way back, he first asked my friend if she wanted to be dropped at her place or anywhere close to public transit. My friend who lived quite a distance from our office shyly responded that she would be fine at the first bus stop on his way. I did not wait for him to ask me the same question; I just offered to get off at the same place and take my own bus home. But he quickly said that it was no problem for him to drop me off at my place. I felt comfortable enough to accept his offer, but I felt bad for leaving my friend behind. Anyhow, I chose to stay and took a ride with him and he used that time to express his interest in me. He asked if I would consider going out with him for the purpose of getting to know each other better. In those days we were not allowed to date and those who chose to go on a date, regardless, were at risk of getting arrested and punished if they got caught. I was among those who chose to disregard such rigid rules and accepted to go out to get to know this man anyway. To be on the safe side, we mostly met up at a restaurant or went out to see a movie together. Sometimes we would go to a nice coffee shop close to where we worked for dessert and talk about what was happening in our lives. Once in a while, we would dare to go out to the park for a walk but we always feared that we might get caught by government agents. It was only safe for people to be out with their spouses, their parents, their siblings and their uncles or aunts. Most people carried their birth certificates in case they were approached by government agents so they could prove they were related. In some instances, we had heard that people who were on a date were captured by government agents and forced to marry each other that day or face prison sentence. Such drastic measures were taken to discourage young people from disobeying the new laws. Come to think of it, it was terrifying to think that they forced those poor souls to get married even if that was the first time they had gone out on a date. How could they spend the rest of their lives together if they knew nothing about one another? Divorce was considered a catastrophe, especially for women, so they were doomed either way.

Luckily, we got a way with it for a long time and were not stopped by agents until one night when we drew too much attention to ourselves. We were taking a leisurely walk and talking about something that had happened earlier; I cannot recall what we were talking about but I remember that we were laughing out loud. A large, black SUV pulled over and cut us off almost as close as if it wanted to run us over. A couple of agents jumped out and shouted at us to move away from each other. Everything happened too fast; it seemed as though I was watching a scene out of an action movie where cops caught up with bank rubbers. My knees were shaking and I could hear my heartbeat. It was obvious that my friend was not doing much better. I was afraid that I might not be able to keep my mouth shut and get us in even bigger problem. I was always vocal and never good at keeping my opinions to myself. I had a feeling that I was not about to be quiet that night either; and I was right. As soon as they approached us, I opened my mouth and told them off. I told them how awful I thought their behaviour was, and how sickening it was that they did all that under the name of Islam. Since I was really upset, I was talking much faster than usual. It was as if I had pushed a play button on a cassette recorder and the stop button was not working. My friend did not have a chance to stop me to do some damage control.

Of course, that did not sit well with the agents and one of them looked at the other and said that he would be taking me in. As soon as my friend heard his comment, he tried to come up with an idea to smooth things out. Fortunately, he found a way to calm them down quickly. He tactfully talked about his involvement, as a volunteer, with the army during Iran and Iraq's war. He then pulled out a certificate, a small card acknowledging his bravery during the war, he had received from the government for his efforts. When they examined the card, they cooled down a bit. My friend was hoping to convince them that they were all on the same side; so perhaps to get them to go easy on us. While they were clearly impressed by my friend, they still looked pretty angry at me for speaking up. They were still debating as to whether or not they should arrest me anyway. My friend was obviously a better diplomat, so he kept talking to them until they agreed to let me go. Before they left, they gave me an irritated look, and promised that next time I would not get off that easy so I better learn to keep my mouth shut. I tried not to laugh since I knew I would not be able to do such a thing! By the same token, I felt relieved at how things had turned out. I was not sure what would have happened to me if I had been arrested that night and sent back to prison again. Or perhaps I did know what could await me and that was why I felt relieved. Regardless, I was impressed by my friend's quick thinking and his ability to negotiate our way out of that big hole.

Over the next few months our initial attraction grew and we became more serious about our relationship. One day as we were having coffee at the local coffee shop he asked me to marry him. He was older than me so he felt it was time for him to settle down. I said yes. I knew that if we got engaged, we could go out freely as we did not have to worry about getting caught. I then informed my family and they agreed to meet him and his family as soon as possible. My dad was surprised since anytime he talked about marriage I walked away indicating I was not ready for it. When I told my family about my friend, their reaction was not favourable. They now knew that he had not gone to university; and that he did not have a stable or well-paid job. They knew he had not come from a wealthy family; so in case we needed financial assistance in the future, they could not help him out in any way. My father said no from the very beginning. Yet, I insisted that I knew what was best for me. Which 19 year old does not think she knows it all? My family wanted me to get involved with someone who could ensure a comfortable life style and a secure financial future for me. There were already men with better financial status who were willing to ask for my hand in marriage. But since money was never a determining factor in my decision making, I informed them that I had already made up my mind and would marry him regardless of their opinion. They finally gave in. Shortly after our discussions, our families met to discuss our possible engagement. It was customary for the groom's family to initiate such contacts as they were supposed to ask my father's permission first. So they visited our home. My father said yes, and events started to unfold very quickly. A month or so after both families met, we got engaged. I was very happy and convinced that I had made the right decision about my future mate and he seemed to be very happy too. I was 19 at the time. We planned our wedding for the summer of the next year when I would turn 20.

While we took that time to plan the wedding, not the marriage unfortunately, I was getting to know him a bit more. His upbringing and family dynamic was just too different from mine. I slowly began to notice that what I had called love could have just been a crush. Day by day I became unsure about my decision but in the beginning I did not dare to admit those feelings even to myself. It was as though I had just taken off my blindfold and could clearly see that we were not meant for each other. To this day, I am not quite sure myself why I felt like that, but I wish I had trusted those feelings. In those days in Iran, perhaps even now in our culture, it was rare that someone would cancel their wedding at the eleventh hour; especially in my case, since I had insisted on marrying him against my family's wishes. I did not have the courage to go back on my word. Plus, they had spent considerable amount of money to plan my wedding and our entire extended family, friends, and neighbours had received the invitations already. I felt helpless. I knew I could not bring myself to put such distress on my family, and so, I kept quiet. Perhaps that was the first time in my life when I had decided not to share my feelings; or maybe the second time since after my release from prison, I never shared my feelings with my family. I decided to go through with the wedding and try to make it work though I was sure I was making a huge mistake. I did not want to let anyone down. The only person who was aware of my doubts was my fiancé who insisted we would be happy together. Perhaps if I had possessed the strength, the wisdom and the common sense that I believe I have today, I would never have gone through with it; for both our sakes. But I was not strong enough. With a heavy heart, I finally said, I do.

CHAPTER 11 -
MY PREGNANCY AND THE
ARRIVAL OF OUR FIRST
BABY:

"Being deeply loved by someone gives you strength, while loving someone deeply gives you courage." (Lao Tzu)

****

I was always unhappy in my marriage. Perhaps I never accepted my husband the way he was, or felt accepted by him in so many ways. Maybe becoming a wife to someone was my way of running away from a devastating reality that I could not live my dream. Perhaps I took the easy way out and got married so as not to have to deal with all the trauma in my life. Now that I was miserable as a wife, I thought that maybe being a mother could help. I thought if I could extend the unconditional love that I so longed for to my baby, perhaps I could become whole again. I felt that by giving what I could not get, I could heal my broken heart. I was wrong again.

I discussed this with my husband and he agreed that it was time for us to have a baby. I went to see a doctor to find out why I was not pregnant yet, now six month into our marriage, even though we were not practicing birth control. My doctor ran some tests and suggested that I should take some pills for a maximum of three months and if by the end of that period I was still not pregnant then he would discuss different options with us. I started to take the pills and at the end of the three months I became pregnant. Everyone was happy to hear the news but part of me was still lost and depressed. It was safe to say that I was probably one of the few women who was truly in despair throughout the pregnancy. I quit my job right away thinking that I might go back and write another test to enter university but instead I just stayed home. My boss and all of my colleagues tried everything to get me to stay but once again, I had made up my mind. However, I thoroughly trained the new lady who was hired to take over my job and months after I left the company I still dropped by constantly to help her out. She had my home number too so she called me quite regularly and I was always more than willing to help her out with her questions. We eventually became best friends since we spent so much time together. But I was comforted in knowing that my boss and the team were in good hands.

I had so much time on my hands. I cried as soon as my husband left for work and at night when he was fast sleep. Now that I was pregnant, I was really missing my mom so much more as I felt that I needed her the most during that time. My step-mother was trying to support me as much as she could but she was not my mom and could never care for me the way my mom could. I promised myself that when my child arrived I would love him or her just the way I wished I would have been loved. And I took comfort in knowing that my baby's love would take away some of my pain. Days turned into weeks and weeks into months as I completed my pregnancy and was ready to deliver my baby. Apparently, my baby was just too big to even turn to get ready for the delivery. My doctor saw me almost every other day for three weeks after the original date of delivery. I had no pain and my baby was still in the same position so he decided to perform a C-section to get the baby out. I had no problem with that since I had heard terrifying stories of natural deliveries and did not think I would be strong enough to go through all that. Besides, there was no indication that I would be able to deliver the baby naturally so I agreed; and I am glad I did. I gave birth to a healthy little boy we named Siavash. I named him after a fearless legendary Persian prince from the earliest days of the Persian Empire who lost his life defending his country. With his thick black hair and big beautiful black eyes, Siavash looked like an angel. He was 10 pounds so my doctor called him a sumo wrestler and confirmed that I would not have been able to give birth to him without C-section no matter how much longer we would have waited.

In a few days I was taking my precious little baby home. I had seen babies around me before but it was not until I had one of my own that I realized the responsibilities that came with it. All I knew was that I loved him and he gave me the reason to want to be alive to see that he was taken care of. I was so attached to him that I would not let him out of my sight. Perhaps I was afraid that like so many other things in life, he would be taken away from me. I became apprehensive and overbearingly protective. Siavash was a good baby but he did not sleep much. As long as the lights were on and we sat with him, he would not cry; but as soon as the lights would go off, he would start to cry. It appeared that I had a tiring journey ahead of me as a mother but no matter how hard things turned out, my love for him grew each day. And I must say that the most enjoyable moments when I truly felt like a great mother was when he looked me in the eye as I breastfed him. I blossomed in seeing him so content and perhaps those were the only moments I felt that I had not failed him as a mother.

As the time went by I still felt depressed and unhappy. I still felt guilty about letting go of my life long dream and settling for being a wife and a mother. Gradually, I noticed the patterns I had developed to run away from my problems. When I was faced with something unpleasant, I detoured and took on something else to distract myself. Slowly, I began to feel regretful to have brought a child to this world that I felt was full of pain and misery. Soon love turned to fear and guilt and it took away so much of my joyous moments with my baby. I knew I had been selfish to bring a child to this world, and I was afraid I could not give him all that he deserved. I became my own worst enemy. I had no self-respect or self-confidence as a mother or as a wife. I always blamed myself for all that had gone wrong in my life and the life of those around me. Unable to forgive myself for all that I held myself accountable for, I started yet another painful chapter in my life.

Chapter 12 -
Leaving Iran:

"The journey of a thousand miles begins with one step." (Lao Tzu)

****

With each passing day, life became much more difficult for us. My husband could not keep a job because of his political beliefs; and I had a baby and could not afford to join the workforce at the time. We finally reached the point were we no longer had the ability to take care of our most basic needs, such as food, rent, or our baby's basic needs. We were quickly running out of options and felt tremendous pressure. My husband and I had casually talked about leaving Iran, that was originally his idea, but I never gave it serious thought. Finally I reached a point where I gave in and agreed to leave Iran with my husband and my one year old son. Our plan was to pack our bags and leave our home to seek refuge somewhere in Europe or North America. We most certainly preferred to immigrate to Canada since we had heard so many wonderful things about life there. My husband had been thinking about it for a while, but I had shown no interest. However, considering all that was happening, I had no choice but to agree with him. So when my older sister, who lived in Turkey at the time, came home for a visit, my husband spoke to her to get a better picture of what could wait for us outside Iran. Throughout my sister's stay with us we had quite a few gatherings. Surrounded by our friends and close family members, we discussed our living conditions and the fact that we were thinking about leaving Iran. Later on, my younger brother managed to go to Turkey and applied to immigrate to Canada. We hoped that someday we could all immigrate to Canada. I had a vision that eventually all of our immediate family members would be reunited in Canada and that was somewhat of a source of comfort for me. However, due to Iran's rocky relationship with the western world, our mission seemed like an impossible one. The senseless war between Iran and Iraq, for almost eight years, made things somewhat difficult as well. Last, but not least, I had heard that people like me, with political prison records, had absolutely no chance of leaving Iran while their names were on the government black list. Plus, there were no legal ways of obtaining a visa to the US, Canada or even Europe directly from Iran. That was why many people travelled to Turkey, Greece, Cypress, and so on, to try to obtain a visa from there. In those days, very few countries were willing to even consider our visa applications. Our government did not want people to leave since it was assumed that they would not be coming back. Regardless, we were determined to find a way, so we took the first step and applied for our passport. Siavash and I did not have a passport but my husband already had a valid one. One day when my sister was taking care of Siavash, I filled out the application, took a photo and visited the passport office in Tehran. My application was accepted and I was asked to visit the office within three weeks. I was very apprehensive since I had a feeling they would be running background checks. To comfort me, some people told me that I since did not spend too long in prison that I might be okay. But, deep down, I knew they were just saying that to make me feel better. Unfortunately I was right! The day arrived that I needed to go back to the passport office. I arrived early morning, took a number and waited for my turn. Shortly after my arrival a young officer called out my number and called me to his kiosk where he was attending to clients. I remember him well since he stood out from most of the other employees. He was polite, good looking and obviously had shaved that very morning. The rest of the male employees looked as though they had not showered for days. Their long beards and mustaches, looked as if no one had attended to them for weeks, and their clothes looked old and wrinkled. Most of the men looked sloppy and unapproachable. Nobody expected much in that regard from women employees. They were not allowed to dress up or to put on make up. They had no choice but to cover their hair, and almost all of them wore lose black garments to cover their entire body. In addition, women could not smile as they greeted people since that was considered improper, and even somewhat sinful behavior. Laugher was certainly out of question since showing off their teeth was considered sinful as well. According to the dictators' interpretation of Islam, women were solely to blame for men's indecent behavior or thoughts. If a man was turned on by a woman that he was not married to, regardless of whether he acted on his desires or not, he had committed a sin. But the woman was to blame for his behavior. So to protect men from giving in to their shameful desires, women had to be restrained in so many ways. After all they argued, men could not control their sexual desires, thoughts or behaviors, when interacting with women, especially attractive ones. Taking pride in one's appearance was considered a sinful and seductive act shunned by our new government. Those who dared to ignore such rules would be punished harshly.

I provided the young officer with my paperwork. He looked up and said hi. I believe in that moment he noticed my apprehension. I quietly asked if my passport was ready. He informed me that I would not be getting my passport today, or any other day. A background check had revealed my prison record and I was not allowed to obtain a passport or leave Iran. I was very upset but tried not to cry in front of him. He could read my face so he tried to be comforting, but I knew there was nothing he or anyone else could do for me. He suggested that, since I had been released from Evin five years ago, I might be able to appeal and get that injunction removed. He provided me with the mailing address and contact names in Evin. The thought of such communication made me feel more apprehensive, but I thanked him and left the office. My family was clearly as disappointed as I, but they encouraged me to take the advice of that young officer and write to have my case reviewed. I finally agreed and wrote a detailed letter explaining that I was now married, had a baby, and wished to visit my sister in Turkey. It took them about three weeks before they responded to me and asked that I meet them in Evin personally for a couple of interviews and to fill out some forms. The thought of going back to Evin was terrifying but since we were determined to leave Iran I finally agreed to meet them at the scheduled date. I was breastfeeding at the time and did not want to leave Siavash behind for an unknown period of time. I was told that the process could take anywhere from a couple of hours, to half a day or more, depending on how busy they were. I decided to take my baby with me. As well, I wanted to portray an image of a completely reformed woman who was leading a new life and content with being a mother and a wife.

Days turned into weeks and before long it was time for my appointment. I got Siavash ready and filled a backpack with necessary items for him, took a cab and left home. On our way to Evin, I was inundated with so many terrifying thoughts about what would happen to us when we got there. I was afraid that this was a trick to get me back, and find an excuse to hold me captive again. I could not bear the thought of losing Siavash and letting him grow up without a mother. I tried to shake all that negativity and to focus on the reason why I was putting myself through this. After a 90 minute ride we finally arrived. I paid the cab, took my baby and walked towards a guard to let him know why I was there. He asked was why I had brought a baby to my appointment. I explained that I had no one to leave him with, and since I was breastfeeding, I could not leave him behind. He shook his head and asked me to follow him in. He left me in a small office and spoke to a few people to explain why I was there. Shortly after I sat down, a couple of people entered the office and spoke to me briefly to inform me of the procedure when attending to cases like mine. They claimed that such reviews would take place at one of their interrogation rooms inside Evin, and that I had to be blindfolded to be taken inside to meet the prosecutor in charge of such cases. My heart sunk when I heard they were going to take us inside Evin, but I knew there was no turning back. I tried to hide my fear from the prison officials who looked indifferent and unfriendly. If I had known about their procedures, I would have either cancelled my appointment or would not have brought my baby along. I thought their administration offices where they handled requests like this were outside the actual prison vicinity. Sadly I was wrong.

I paused for a moment and asked, "how could I carry my baby and walk through the corridors with blindfold on? I hoped they would make an exception in my case and ask the prosecutor to come to me in the office instead of us making the trip inside Evin. With a firm yet indifferent tone, they replied that they could not break the protocols and that I should have thought about all that before bringing my baby to prison. I knew better than to discuss this issue any further so I kept quiet. I only asked if the guard would be a bit more patient as I needed to walk carefully to make sure I would not fall and hurt my baby. The guard said that he would do his best not to rush me through but that I could not walk too slowly. Walking through those corridors, in darkness, with so many curves and turns, while carrying a one year old baby, and a heavy backpack, was not an easy task. My knees were shaking. I could hear my heartbeat. I was petrified for my baby's safety. The extra pressure from the tightly fastened blindfold was causing me to feel dizzy. Siavash held on to me so tightly that I could hear his heartbeat. He tried to remove my blindfold any chance he got. If all of that was not so very scary and sad, it would have been a bit funny. I did not want more trouble so I whispered in his ears begging him leave it alone. At one, he could say a few words. He was mumbling something trying to ask what was happening. He sounded playful as if he took all this to be a funny make believe game. While I tried not to laugh out loud, I kept asking him to keep quiet. Siavash would listen and stop for a minute, but after a while he would start again. He was still curious, and each time he successfully pulled up my blindfold, he stared at me chuckling. At least he distracted me while I was blaming myself for bringing him there with me. I thought I had been the worst mother in the entire world to have put my own flesh and blood in such a dangerous position. Flooded by fear, shame and guilt, I only thought of the worst case scenarios. These scenarios were not helping my sanity. We must have walked about 15 to 20 minutes, but it seemed like a lifetime before I was finally told to stop and enter a room. As the guard left locking the door behind him, he said I could remove my blindfold and wait until someone came in. I quickly removed my blindfold and saw that I was placed in a private cell, not an office. I felt even more apprehensive, thinking that they might have planned this all along. I knew that if they wanted to hold me there indefinitely they did not need a reason, nor did they have to explain themselves to anyone. Feeling helpless, I tried to redirect my attention. I decided to change Siavash's diaper and breastfeed him as he seemed to be a bit restless. As well, I felt that I could use some rest myself since I was tired of carrying him and the heavy bag through the long dark corridors. I was thankful for our chance to unwind so I could connect with Siavash and try my best to make him feel safe once again. I suddenly remembered the time that Iran was under constant bomb attack from Iraq. Tehran was targeted and hit quite a few times; each time it felt as if an earthquake with an 8.0 magnitude had struck. Even with all that intense shaking and unimaginably loud noises, when the bombs hit somewhere close to our home, Siavash never cried. Loud sirens would go off notifying that bombers, Iraq's military aircrafts, were about to attack our city any minute. I never feared for my life but I wanted to protect my baby. I would remove Siavash from his bed, distance ourselves from the windows and start singing a lullaby to him holding him tight in my arms. With his big brown eyes, he would look at me as though he wondered if all was well. I would give him few kisses while promising to keep him safe and would smile at him as if nothing was wrong. A look of satisfaction on Siavash's face would give me the strength to keep going. I would take comfort in knowing that he felt safe in my arms. Those memories helped me calm down a bit and help Siavash feel more comfortable as well.

We must have waited for another 20 minutes or so when I heard the door being unlocked and a man's voice telling me to put my blindfold on. He gave me some papers and asked me to start writing. But before he left, he asked that I hand over my baby to him. I almost had a heart attack; with a shaky voice I asked why he wanted to take Siavash away. He replied, with a firm voice, that I had a lot to do and the baby would be a distraction to me. He assured me that he'd be fine and asked what his name was. He promised that they would play with him while I was filling out the paperwork. I told the guard that my baby's name was Siavash. He asked why I had not picked a religious name like Mohammed, Ali or Hussein. I bit my tongue and kept quiet. I had a feeling that they would not have liked my answer. Instead, I kissed Siavash and told him that he would be spending some time with that man until I was done. I am sure he did not understand what I was saying to him but he kept quiet as I handed him over to the guard. Siavash had always been too attached to me. For the past year I had not been able to leave him with anyone to go out and run errands. So I was pretty sure that he would cry as soon as he was separated from me and the guards would have to bring him back. To my utter amazement, he left without any objection as though he was excited to be apart from me for the first time in his life. I was disappointed that I was out of excuses to keep him next to me, but I was also proud of him for being such an angel. That pushed me to fill out the paperwork and answer all of their questions as quickly as possible. I was told they would check up on me in about an hour or so, and if I was done, then they would take the papers and bring my baby to me. When I finished filling out the forms and responding to questions, I put them aside hoping a guard who was assigned to check up on me would see it and know that I was done. Finally, after waiting for several minutes, a guard came in and collected the paperwork. I remained seated facing the walls. I was told to stay in that position until further notice. As he was leaving, I asked if my baby was doing okay and when I would get him back. He responded enthusiastically that he had been keeping him busy in the office and everyone loved playing with him. He continued on to say that he was such a good baby and never cried. He closed the door and came back with Siavash few minutes after that. I was excited to hold my wonderful baby in my arms again, and I could tell that he was happy to see me too. Soon after, another guard came in and told me to grab my stuff and put my blindfold on so he could escort us outside of Evin. I was told that I would be notified of the result in a few weeks. I was ecstatic with relief when I finally got a cab and was on my way home. At home, everyone was anxiously waiting my return, to have my baby and me back safe and sound. It took about three weeks before I got the letter that my request had not been approved. I was outraged to know that I had put Siavash and I through so much distress and nothing had come of it. Yet, I knew we had to find a way out. I promised myself not to give up until we safely left Iran. Finally, our efforts paid off. We got connected with a guy named "Hassan" whom we had heard could help us obtain a passport despite our circumstances. He told us that we could play the system to our advantage and work around their rules. My husband and I were lost; we asked for more explanation. "Hassan" told us that since I was married, my husband could apply for a family passport under his name. He indicated that perhaps my husband should not apply for this passport in Tehran, but he should travel to another city, "Babol", about a five or six hour drive from Tehran and fill out the application from there. Of course there was some risk associated with such actions, but we felt that we had no other viable option. He was right in suggesting that my husband apply for a family passport. Women were treated as though they were second class citizens. Those who were married were mostly identified as someone's wife. As a married woman, there would not be much emphasis on my maiden name. Those who were issuing passports would more carefully investigate the last name of the head of our family, my husband. But in order to apply for a passport in "Babol", we had to come up with an address to prove that we lived there. Our contact took care of that as well as he had close relatives who lived in that city. He prepared a false employment letter for my husband to prove that he was working in that city. For the first time in a long while we were able to see the light at the end of tunnel. We were advised that upon obtaining our passport, we should arrange to leave Iran by crossing Turkey's borders via car or bus. He absolutely forbade us to fly out of Iran since the likelihood of a more thorough investigation was much higher at the airports. I knew he was certainly right. I remembered what the good looking officer, who worked at Tehran's passport office, had told me. He said my name was among those at every airport in the country, who were not permitted to leave Iran. We trusted "Hassan" in helping us obtain our passport, since he had proven his credibility to us.

Things went as planned. We were granted a family passport and now it was time to follow through on the rest of our plans. No one else could know about this to guarantee our safe departure from Iran. In front of friends and neighbors, we pretended that we were about to leave for a month vacation in Turkey to visit my sister and brother. As part of our plan, we left our apartment untouched and did not attempt to sell any of our belongings. We reserved a cabin on a train leaving Tehran to Tabriz, a city in the Northern part of Iran, closer to Turkey's borders. After our arrival in Tabriz, we had to take a bus to leave for Turkey. My older brother offered to accompany us from Tehran to Tabriz to make sure that we, in fact, got on a bus to Turkey, meaning our family passport passed inspection by the government agents. Having my brother with us meant a lot to me. I knew we had someone to take care of Siavash if we got caught or arrested at the borders. Someone who could let our families know what had happened to us if we did not make it.

It was a nice spring day when we finally got ready to leave for Turkey. I had been feeling anxious and sad now that I knew we might actually be able to leave Iran. There were many reasons for my inner turmoil and apprehension, but among those one stood out and kept me doubtful of my decision to leave Iran. Leaving my 11-year old sister behind was breaking my heart into pieces. We were extremely close and almost inseparable ever since our mom died. I was more than a sister to her. I was not sure how she was going to handle my leaving. I was certain that being apart from her would be yet another of the most difficult things I had to deal with in my life. I felt guilty and ashamed as though I was betraying my sister in so many ways. I was dying inside knowing that I could not take her with me. She had lost her mom at such young age and now she was going to lose me too. It was not enough that she had lost me to a husband and a baby, now she was being left behind while I planned my escape from Iran. I remembered how sad my sister was on my wedding day; how much she and I both cried. She was afraid she would not get to see me and that things would change between us. With a heavy heart and tearful eyes I had promised her that nothing would change between us; that my new home was also hers. And now I was breaking my promise. I was leaving her just like our mom left her. What words would be adequate enough to explain to an eleven-year old why she was losing those she loved? So I did not say much fearing I would break down and cry in front of her on the day we were saying goodbye. She came to the train station to see me off. I remembered how she looked at me as though it was yesterday. Her big brown eyes spoke of much agony and distress but, much like me, she pulled herself together and did not cry in front of me. That day at the train station I left the best part of me behind. Indeed I was not whole anymore.

Separating from my baby sister was the one of the biggest disappointments and heartbreaks I had to endure, but that was not all of it. Deep down regardless of all that happened to me, I did not want to leave my country. I did not want to leave all that I had ever known. I was terrified of the uncertain future that would unfold before us as we set foot in a strange country. We did not have much money. We were not sure how we would take care of our basic needs, much less our fifteen-month old baby's needs. I felt as though I was trapped in a dark cave not able to find a way out; hardly able to breathe. But there was no time to fall apart now. The plans were in motion. For Siavash's sake I held myself together and kept going. I never forgave myself for leaving my baby sister behind, regardless of the fact that there were no other options available to us.

The train ride was a quiet one. I hardly spoke, and since I felt sick, I took Siavash in my arms and slept almost all the way through. Upon arrival to Tabriz, we took a room at a motel close to the bus station as our bus was leaving early the next day. We were all nervous; terrified at the thought that we might caught at the border. Early the next day, we all got up to got ready for the bus station. Once there, we said our goodbyes, but my brother assured us that he would not leave until he was sure that we had safely boarded the bus. As he was watching us from the distance, agents were going through our bags as part of their routine checks. Suddenly, we remembered that my prison record, a small pocket size certificate I had obtained from Evin on the day of my release, was in one of our suitcases. My husband acted quickly and got to the paper before the agents. I don't know how he pulled it off, but he was able to grab it and run it to my brother. Pretending that he was saying goodbye one last time, he then quickly whispered to my brother to mail that paper to my sister's address in Turkey. I almost had a heart attack. But I truly believe that God took care of us at that moment. Miraculously, we got away with it, and were cleared to leave Iran.

As soon as the bus left, we both let out a loud sigh thanking God for giving us a second chance in life. Our bus ride to Turkey was nice and Siavash, as always, was an angel and loved by everyone in the bus. And so that was how we finally fled Iran in search of a home someplace where we did not to have to live in constant fear.

Chapter 13 –
In Turkey for 4 months –
Moving on to Greece

When you come to the end of all the lights you know and you are about
to step off into the darkness of the unknown, faith is knowing one of two
things will happen:
There will be something solid to stand on, or you'll be taught how to fly!
(Unknown source)

****

Upon our arrival in Istanbul, we were greeted by my older sister who had
been living there for a couple of years. She had lived in Turkey hoping to
find a place to which she could immigrate and call home later on. My
younger brother was also in Turkey waiting for his immigration papers
to Canada to be processed. I could not imagine what would happen to
us in Turkey if we did not have them to support us. My sister knew her
way around and had quite a few friends. Her place was too small so we
could not stay with her but she arranged for us to stay with couple of her
friends instead. Though we were comfortable at her friends' place, after
a while we decided to find another place to live since we were not sure
how much longer we would be staying in Turkey. Pretty soon, my sister
was able to help us find a cheap hotel close to where she lived so we could
move out of her friends' house. Siavash and I were very comfortable in

that motel as people who worked there took care of us as though we were family. The staff loved Siavash who warmed up to them pretty quickly. They spoiled him just as much as our own family in Iran would have. Every day they would take him out to buy him chocolates and other yummy treats. Since Siavash loved Coke, they would serve it to him without charging us. Siavash also liked playing with ants. A few of the people there would take him out on a daily basis, gather some ants in a container, and bring it to the hotel so he could play with them on a table. I remember one night Siavash was quite sick and my husband was out looking to meet with smugglers. I did not want to call my sister since she did not have a car. Fortunately, I did not have to, as the staff always checked up on Siavash and I before we went to bed. That night, when they saw him feverish and throwing up, they drove us to the nearest clinic; waited for the doctor to see him; took me to the pharmacy to buy his medication, and then drove me back to the hotel. Siavash was not doing too well and I was up most of the night, leaving the door half open. I had quite a few visitors who checked up on us to see if we needed more assistance. I never forgot what they did for us that night and how they cared for Siavash when he needed it the most. Perhaps they were our guardian angels disguised as hotel workers, keeping a close eye on us, protecting us from any harm.

Shortly after our arrival, we started discussing how to immigrate to Canada. We were advised that applying for immigration from Turkey could take quite a long time. Considering the challenging living conditions in Istanbul, and our terrible financial circumstances, we decided to find an alternative country to temporarily call home while waiting for our immigration papers. Greece was highly recommended to us at the time. We heard that my husband could easily find work and provide for his family, but we had no way of legally entering Greece. We began to explore illegal ways to find refuge at the United Nation office in Athens. We were told that if we did not get caught as we tried to enter Greece, the rest of our journey would be without any challenge.

Through my sister's acquaintances we got connected to people who would charge to smuggle us to different countries. We were told that getting us to Greece was like a walk in a park for them. I did not have much understanding of how smugglers operated and was not aware it was so dangerous. I learned that they would make a fake passport and/

or travel document, and pick a specific date and time to send people off using busses, cruise ships, trains or plains. I also found out why they had to be specific about times. The smugglers had contacts which were paid off to look the other way when they recognized the fake travel documents. And they had to work with their contacts' schedules to ensure nothing would go wrong at the borders. They shared a percentage of the money, they received from their clients, to pay off their contacts. In return, they guaranteed their customers an easy way out of Turkey and into countries like Canada, Germany, Sweden, Norway, Denmark and other countries accepting refugees. Considering what was going on in Iran, our people were more than willing to pay the "people smugglers" handsomely to find refuge somewhere in Europe or North America. Of course there were quite a few people from other troubled countries along with Iranians, so the market for such services was quite hot.

Ironically, Istanbul seemed to be the right place to get connected with people who made their living as smugglers. So while we stayed at that motel, we kept an eye out to find the one that we could trust to some degree. We had heard horrifying stories about smugglers who betrayed their clients; so we had a hard time finding the one we could trust. A lot of people had lost all their life savings and had nowhere to turn. After all, to whom could they complain? We even heard some people were robbed and murdered along the way. We were very apprehensive. Considering all those risks, we took our time to meet with a few smugglers, or their representatives, hoping to choose right. We were young and trusting, not prepared to deal with predators who stopped at nothing to get their hands on some money.

Thankfully, I was able to learn the language very quickly. In less than four months I was able to understand, read, write and speak Turkish. I could easily understand most conversations and while speaking, I was able to articulate my message clearly. I was not even sure why I showed that much interest in learning Turkish; but in time, I understood the importance of knowing the language, especially under such special circumstances. Our options were to get to Greece by air, sea or land, but since we could not afford air travel, we were left with the other two options. I felt sick even considering such risky and dangerous options, but deep down I knew there were no other possibilities for us. A week or two prior to finding the right contact, that got us talking to the smugglers we finally picked, we met an Iranian family in the motel. They were in Turkey to find a way to go to Greece, since the gentleman's brother was already in Greece, and registered with the UN. "Nasrin" and "Reza" looked quite a few years older than us and they were expecting their first baby. They both seemed warm and friendly so we quickly became such close friends that we shared our plans with them. They were ecstatic to hear about our plans, and said that if it worked out, they would love to take the same route with us. I was happy to hear that. Two other adults travelling with us made me feel a whole lot safer. Both "Reza" and "Nasrin" were tall and well built, and looked much stronger than my husband and I. Unfortunately, they had even less money than us; so unless a miracle happened, they could not accompany us. My husband and I trusted them enough to agree to lend them some of the money. In return, "Reza" promised to take us to his brother's house, and got the money he owed us from him. We told them that we would not over welcome our stay, and as soon as we get the money back, we would get a room at a cheap motel in Athens. So, with that couple on our side, we continued on our search until we finally met a woman who claimed she could help us with our mission. She claimed that she knew of a few people who could smuggle us to Greece in a boat. She seemed genuine and empathetic, and assured us that this way would be almost as easy as flying out to Greece. She made us feel really comfortable. She said that the smugglers would drive us to a designated spot where a boat would be waiting. She said that there was absolutely no risk involved, and no chance of getting caught by Turkish or Greek law enforcement. In fact, she claimed that the border agents/ gate keepers were already bribed so we had absolutely nothing to worry about. What more could we ask for, we thought? So we happily paid her the money she asked for and agreed upon a date for our departure. Since we had little money left to spend, after paying the smugglers and lending the money to our friends, we asked her to arrange to get us out of Turkey as soon as possible.

On a hot summer night in late July about a week after, around 10 pm, we packed our bags and left the hotel with our friends. My sister was there to say good bye to us when the three smugglers showed up to pick us up. We took a big suitcase and packed all of our clothes since the lady had assured us that we could take what we wanted. We also packed a couple of small bags containing diapers and Siavash's clothing. I also had a small album with me that contained all of my mom's photos, my own photos when I was a baby and my sisters and brothers' photos. That was worth more to me than anything else in the world. By carrying that album with me, I was carrying a small piece of my real home, Iran. While I was in Istanbul, the album was always with me no matter where I went. I kept it in a small backpack that I carried with me that night. I did not even feel comfortable leaving it on one of our big suitcases in case, for some reason, we were to lose it.

We were finally ready to leave but saying goodbye to my sister was very painful for me. While she cried, I cried with her as I gave her a hug. She was worried about us, especially for my baby. Siavash looked apprehensive when he saw us crying. He held on to me tightly trying to find some comfort. As we took our seats, the minivan took off. It passed through the busy streets of Istanbul which were still lively at that time of night. I quietly stared through the windows at people who were still up and around. The first hour of our drive was not too bad, but as we moved further away from the city, there was nothing but darkness, barren dirt roads, and flat lands. There were no other cars. The road was completely dark and we could not see any sign of life of any kind. From time to time, we heard a cry that sounded like the growling of a wolf or a coyote. A couple of hours passed and we had barely spoken with one another. We could smell the fear eating away at each and every one of us, including Siavash. As I held him quietly in my arms, I listened to the smugglers as they spoke among themselves. I began to get a really bad feeling about all of that. I could not shake off such feelings so I felt even more apprehensive. After about two hours or so, around 12 am, the mini van finally stopped. It looked as though we were in the middle of nowhere. We looked around anxiously to find our boat, but to our utmost dismay the only thing we could see was pitch black sky and barren roads for miles. We were told to get out of the van and take our stuff with us. The driver said that he was leaving us with the other two guides; he was going back to Istanbul. Since I was the only one who knew Turkish, I asked when our boat would be there, and that was when we were told the whole truth. The driver, who seemed older than the other two, looked puzzled, as though he had no idea what I was talking about. I told him what their woman accomplice, had promised us. I thought he must have had us mixed up with a different group set up to travel this route. Little did I know, there was no other route, and no other group of people. Their operation was a fraud. We were being dumped in a remote place far from anyone or anything we knew.

When I heard the driver's version of our planned trip to Greece I almost passed out. It was as though I got hit on the head with a baseball bat. Feeling dizzy and nauseous, I sat down quickly as I felt I might throw up any minute. I was furious to finally realize how badly we have been deceived; and scared to death for Siavash's safety.

The driver made it clear there was no boat, and that we had to make this illegal entry over land. He explained that for the next couple of hours we were going to hike, run, briskly walk or crawl, depending on what our guides asked us to do. We were told that there might be times when we needed to lie down so quiet as though we were playing dead. The smugglers claimed that slightest movement could alert Greece's border agents which would be a disaster for all of us.

Before leaving, the driver looked at us and said: "one more thing; you cannot take anything except couple of light backpacks that are not too heavy for you to carry." I was really upset that he did not say anything to us in Istanbul so we could leave our suitcase with my sister instead of lugging it with us. He looked indifferent and cold, and after a brief pause, he suggested that perhaps he could help us out. He said that instead of us dumping our suitcase in the middle of nowhere, he was willing to take it back to Istanbul and see that my sister gets it. We knew we had no other option but to accept his offer and hand in our suitcase to him. Time was running out and we had to do what we were told before the driver left. I quickly took some things out of our big suitcases and put them into our backpacks. It was at that point that I took out my family album from my backpack, since it was too heavy, and placed it inside the suitcase the driver was taking back. The thought of losing that album troubled me; yet I tried to convince myself that my sister would mail it to us as soon as we got settled in Greece. When we were ready, the driver put our suitcase inside the van and assured us that my sister would get them by tomorrow. As I saw him driving off, I became even more nervous. We were now left alone with two young guides who seemed a bit odd. I immediately had second thoughts about our decision to stay. I wondered if we had made a mistake and perhaps we should have gone back to Istanbul. Yet, my gut was telling me that we had no other option but to move forward. Even if we got back to Istanbul there was no guarantee that we could ever find that lady smuggler; and even if we did find her, we knew she would never return our money. It was obvious why she had lied to us. Had she told us the truth, we would never have agreed to pay her off and use this route to Greece.

I asked my husband for a cigarette. He looked at me in disbelief since he knew how much I hated smoking. Even the smell of a lit cigarette would make me sick; and perhaps smoking was one of the biggest reasons my husband and I argued in the past. But I was deeply troubled. I thought smoking might help calm me down, even if temporarily, and in a strange way, it did! What frightened me the most was the impossible task of making sure my 18-month old baby would keep quiet at all times. I was petrified of what those ruthless smugglers might do to him if he suddenly cried. It was obvious that they only cared about themselves and would stop at nothing to ensure they were not caught. I was afraid for our safety; especially Siavash's since I could see them capable of the unthinkable. For all we knew, they could be thieves and murderers who had plotted to get rid of us in the middle of nowhere. I only prayed that they would kill me first so I would not get to see what they would do to Siavash. A violent chill came over my body as I pictured such a tragic end for us. Not knowing if we would survive such an ordeal, I decided not to give up for the sake of Siavash. It took every fiber of my being to hold myself strong and not to scream or cry. I knew I could not break down; not then and not like that. I pulled myself together, put up a strong front and pretended that I was okay with this plan. I behaved as though I trusted our guides so much and told them that I was thinking of referring some of our friends, who were still in Turkey, to them. I explained that my initial reaction was because of my own misunderstanding, and perhaps, as a result of not knowing Turkish too well. I never let on how much I knew, so they could comfortably talk to each other in front of me. Now I was thankful I showed so much interest in learning Turkish during our short stay in Istanbul!

Everyone else in our small group looked frightened, too. I suggested that they hide their fear as much as possible, not to make the smugglers feel more powerful. I said that any sign of suspicion and mistrust could actually encourage them to harm us. "Reza" said that he was carrying a knife in his pocket. He promised that he would keep an eye on any suspicious activity without drawing too much attention to himself. I must admit that having them with us comforted me. I thanked him, turned around and sat closer to the smugglers to listen in on their conversation. I waited until they stopped talking and then asked, pretending to be enthusiastic about the whole thing, what was next for us. I was informed that after couple of hours of hiking, they would get us to a truck waiting somewhere in the middle of the road. At that point, they would say goodbye to us, and the truck driver, another one of their accomplices, would take us to a small town inside Greece close to the railroads. We would then spend the night with yet another person who was working with the truck driver. We would then be dropped off the next morning to catch a train leaving for Athens. If we did not get caught on the train, then we had made it; and if we did get caught, no one could help us anymore. I had heard all that I could handle for now so I thanked them politely and excused myself to go back to my husband, my baby and our friends. While I held Siavash in my arms tightly, I shared what I had heard from the smugglers about our plans. Considering all the obstacles we had to overcome, I believed only a miracle could keep us from any harm. I quietly prayed for the safety of my innocent baby.

We were still where the van had dropped us off. The guides had a specific time in mind to get us moving. We had to wait patiently until we had been given the go ahead. Finally, after what seemed like a life time, we were told to get our stuff and follow them. One guide walked ahead of us and one walked behind us. I did not want to let go of Siavash. While I carried on one of our backpacks, I held Siavash in my arms so that he was facing me. I knew I could always comfort him when he was scared. All I had to do was to hold him tight in my arms while looking into his eyes. More than ever I needed to be there for him. My husband took the other two heavy bags we had brought with us so his hands were full as well. "Reza" and "Nasrin" did not have too much so it was easier for them to move. But Nasrin was pregnant and a bit too heavy to keep up the pace. While our heavy loads were preventing us from keeping up with the guides, we were afraid to walk too fast since we did not know where we were putting our feet. In such darkness, we could have stepped on a snake and been bitten or fallen into a hole and broken our bones. So while our guides were threatening to leave us if we did not move faster, we tried to be very cautious as well. I was particularly fearful of falling and hurting my baby so I paid close attention, as much as I could, to where I was walking. I was absolutely terrified since we had been warned about wolves, coyotes and other dangerous animals we might encounter along the way. As though all that tension was not enough, suddenly, we were asked to run as fast as we could. To say that running with a big baby and a heavy backpack seemed next to impossible is an understatement. I was out of breath and light headed. I feared I was going to faint any minute. My knees were shaking, my muscles were burning, and every bone in my body hurt. I did not think I could go on. At some point, few minutes into our running, I stopped to take a breath. Immediately, one of the guides ran toward me. I told him he could leave me and move on, but he assured me that I would not last an hour alone out there. For Siavash's sake, I got up and started running again. Though the guards were not carrying a heavy load of their own, none of them offered a helping hand with our bags. I could hear my heartbeat as if it was going to fly out of my chest. My legs were so sore I feared they would just stop working any minute. From time to time I begged the guides to let us rest for a minute. While they could not be too accommodating, they allowed us the odd minute here and there to catch our breaths. I must admit that I was losing hope that we would survive; yet since I had vowed to keep Siavash safe, I kept going.

Siavash was petrified and he did not take his eyes off me. With his big beautiful brown eyes he stared at me as though he was asking if everything was okay. With a cry of agony in my heart, I would kiss him while promising him that all was well. I knew he could sense something was wrong. I whispered to him to stay quiet for now.

I found it especially difficult when we had to crawl and use our elbows to carry ourselves forward. With a big baby and a heavy backpack, that sounded like a mission that would not be possible. To protect Siavash when we crawled, I placed him on my back and carried the backpack in front of me. Siavash was not happy with that arrangement since he could not look into my eyes. I promised that this was only temporary. Soon I felt as though I was fainting. I laid down for a second. Each time we heard a growling of an animal in the middle of the pitch black barren fields, Siavash held on to me tighter. I could hear his heartbeat as he whispered "mom." He wanted to make sure I was still there with him. I kissed his hands and told him that was just a dog, and that all was well. One of the guides finally felt sorry for me and offered to carry my backpack for a bit. I felt so relieved and gladly handed it over.

We must have carried on for at least two hours before we finally stopped. Fear was nibbling at us. We were all hungry, dirty and in great physical pain. We were relieved to rest for a while and I was able to breastfeed Siavash and change his diaper. The guides informed us that the truck should arrive within half an hour or so. We were still in Turkey and the truck would get us through the border and into a small town in Greece. Thankfully the plan was that the guides would stay with us until their contact showed up. All that did not sound too bad. We figured we would be taking a comfortable ride into Greece and that the worst was behind us! Well, we spoke too soon. As soon as the truck arrived, and we were informed of our seating arrangements, I felt ready to give up and call it quits. The truck driver explained to us that since the truck would be thoroughly searched before entering Greece, we had to hide under a false floor beneath the actual seats until we got to that small town. Well, one glance at the false floor was enough to send me in a state of frenzy. I almost shouted at him asking how he expected us to get inside that hole and risk the life of our innocent baby. He responded, it was either that, or we could stay where we were to be attacked by wild animals or get caught by Turkish or Greek law enforcement officials. I was disgusted and sick to my stomach, yet I knew we were out of options. The driver of the truck assured me that he had done this before and no one had suffocated through that. It was hard to believe a word he was saying since it seemed that we were being buried alive in a shallow grave. What looked like a metal coffin had a few small holes to let the air in. We were to lie down inside that shallow grave and keep quiet until the truck successfully passed the border. He would then let us out that hole so we could sit in the back of the truck. We finally agreed to get in. We needed to lie down close to one another to fit in the space. I went in first, and as I laid down, though I was very petite, my face almost touched the ceiling/roof of that false floor. I asked my husband to give me Siavash, and after that he got in himself. That was when they locked the doors. I tried talking to Siavash to keep his mind off of what was going on; I also asked him to close his eyes, keep still, and not make any noise. As terrified as he looked, he listened to me and kept quiet.

The truck, inside and out, was very dirty. I worried that dirt would get into my baby's eyes through the holes. I stretched and held my hand over his eyes not touching them. He was listening and had his eyes closed. With a bit of noise, he would open his eyes to see what was happening. If it was not for him being such an angel, we would have gotten caught for sure when the truck was being thoroughly checked at the border. Fearing the worst, I listened to his breaths to make sure he was still breathing.

Our friends had a different hiding spot inside that truck where they could sit. They were not as thin as we were, so they could not fit inside the same false floor that we were in. Neither of us knew how the others were doing until the truck successfully passed through the check point at the border, after which the truck suddenly stopped. Thankfully they let us out of that hole. We could finally take our seats inside the truck. I was overcome with joy. With tears in my eyes I held Siavash in my arms and thanked God for keeping him safe. The worst was behind us at least for the time being. After a while we were dropped off in a small town, a hamlet, in Greece. The truck driver's contact in that town opened his home to us and prepared a room for us to sleep in. Because we had a baby, our hosts gave us a room to sleep in, but, they had to put our friends in a shed. They brought some tomatoes, feta cheese and bread that we quite enjoyed. Siavash enjoyed the food as well. Though I was breastfed him, he was still really hungry; and shortly after we all ate, the three of us fell sleep quickly.

The next morning, as the sun was slowly rising, we got up and had breakfast. Afterwards, when we got reunited with our friends, we talked about how comfortable we were and how well we slept. Unfortunately their stay was not quite as comfortable as ours. They complained of their sleeping arrangements and the uncomfortable space in that shed. Apparently they hardly got any sleep through the night. Shortly after we were reunited with our friends, we were driven to a train station as previously planned. Since we did not have tickets, we were let out close to a stop that was in the middle of nowhere and least likely to have agents checking for tickets. The place we were dropped off looked more like the Sahara. We were not sure if walking along that path would get us to the train. Thankfully for us, after about fifteen minutes of walking, we saw the stop and a couple of people who were waiting for a train to Athens. After a while the train arrived and we got in through one of the back doors. Most Greeks knew English so it was not too difficult for us to carry on basic introductory conversations and act like tourists taking a small town's path to get to Athens. Since we had a baby and a pregnant woman with us we looked less suspicious. We got on the train with no problem and planned to give the conductors money instead of tickets when they approached our booth. We were told to pretend that we did not have Drachma on us, but only US dollars to buy the tickets. We hoped they would be okay with that instead. It worked. We slept almost all the way to Athens which was about eight hours. It seemed as though our long and terrifying journey to Greece was coming to an end. No words could describe how we all felt at the moment when the train finally reached Athens.

Now it was time to think about where we would stay. As per our agreement with our friends, we were to collect the money owed to us from "Reza's" brother and check into a motel that night. However, when we got off the train, "Reza" insisted that we spend that night at his brother's place. We were tired and hungry and did not know the language or anyone else in that city, so we gratefully accepted his offer. "Reza" called his brother asking for direction to his place. Soon we were sitting in a bus and on our way. We were greeted by a young couple with a small baby boy who seemed almost the same age as Siavash. It was almost dinner time so we all washed up and got ready to eat. Siavash was quite happy to be washed up and get into some clean clothes. The diaper rash he had developed during our trip was really bothering him. We now had the baby rash ointment to apply to affected areas and provide him with some relief. After he was all taken care of, we sat down and chatted after dinner for a couple of hours and then got ready to go to bed. Before falling asleep that night, my husband and I agreed we would leave right after breakfast the next day after collecting our money.

The next morning we woke up and were greeted again by our hosts. They had set up a very nice breakfast table for us. After I attended to Siavash and finished eating breakfast, I looked for an opportunity to be alone with my husband and asked him if he had a chance to talk about money yet. "Not yet;" he said but he promised that while he was out with them to find a job he would bring that up. He was told that finding work at restaurants or construction sites would be quite feasible. The second day passed. We still had not left our friends' house. The longer we stayed on, the more uncomfortable I was beginning to feel. They seemed very different from us, and I sensed they had old fashioned ideas. Men in that family had no respect for their wives, and partnership between a husband and wife sounded too ridiculous to them. I was beginning to find a lot of their behaviour unacceptable and even damaging to our family. The men did the talking and the women were treated like maids. Since I did not grow up like this, I felt like an outsider. No matter how I acted, or what I talked about, I felt I was being judged by that family in some way. My husband was ridiculed by the men. They thought he was not enough of a man since he was helping me out with our baby. As far as they were concerned, men only got women pregnant; the rest was not up to them. They believed women were created to serve men and raise babies. Where I had come from men partnered with their wives in all that they did, including caring for babies.

I once saw "Reza's" sister-in-law cooking while holding her baby in her arms. I asked if I could help out in anyway suggesting that I could either take care of the baby or help her in the kitchen. She declined my offer claiming that she would be okay handling all that on her own. She said that her husband never helped her out at home so she was used to taking care of all the chores and the baby. I was truly puzzled. All that meant, to me, that she was endangering the life of her baby. What if the baby got burned by hot oil or boiling water? It was not like her husband was not available. He was just sitting on a comfortable chair on the balcony enjoying the nice sunny day; so I could not think why this was such a big deal for him to handle the baby while his wife was cooking. I was now curious to find out why the women in that family put up with such all that nonsense; so one day when the men were out looking for work, I brought it up. This was just to satisfy my own curiosity; my intention was not to cause any problem or to encourage those women to rebel against their husbands. At first, they explained how young they were when their marriages were arranged; and how they parents led similar lives. As much as they were trying to convince me that they were okay with the way things were, I could hear profound sadness in their voice. It felt more like they were trying to convince themselves and not me, but they wanted to be heard and share their worries. I could not help but share what I thought of a partnership within a marriage. I suggested to them that both parties were equal partners and there to support one another in any way possible. In my eyes, neither were allowed to bully or belittle each other; nor was physical or verbal abuse allowed. I talked about my dad as an example of a man who partnered with my mom in all aspects of their lives including sharing responsibilities in raising their children. When I finished talking, I saw those two women look at me with their mouths wide open. Perhaps they would have looked less surprised if an alien just got dropped off at their door step.

I could not wait to leave that place. Not only I was appalled by their manners, but I also felt that they were influencing my husband negatively. In about three days, he had become self-conscious, and was trying not to attend to our baby when others were around. To make matters worst, every time I asked my husband when we would leave he would come up with what sounded like an excuse to me. I believe it was on the fourth day when I gave my husband an ultimatum - I would be leaving with or without him; and did not care if I had any money in my pocket. I just could not stand being there anymore especially after the last incident. That day, just before lunch, our hosts had a fight. "Reza's" brother grabbed a metal coat hanger, took his wife into a room and started beating her up viciously. We could hear her scream, but no one was going to help her. Her heartbreaking screams brought back horrifying memories of my time in Evin. Angry and traumatized, I covered Siavash's ears when I saw him terrified. Later, I found out that the only reason she was beaten was that she asked her husband to hold the baby for a few minutes so she could finish cooking. After the husband was tired of beating her up, he came out of the room. Immediately after, I saw the wife following him outside and begging for forgiveness. It was sickening to witness such humiliation. I could not understand why the prey was begging the predator for forgiveness. Perhaps I could never understand them but I slowly began to realize that their marriage was the way it was. By signing a marriage contract, she had become her husband's property. He could treat her anyway he saw fit without any consequences.

He was still angry. He kept cursing at her to leave him alone or she receive more beatings, but the wife knew that if he did not forgive her at that moment, there would be more abuse later on. To show her loyalty to him and to show that she had no problem remaining his slave, she told her husband about the conversation we had earlier. In fact, she bent the truth so much, that the husband thought I was planning to turn his wife against him. He approached my husband and rudely asked him to leave because he was not man enough to control his woman, me. As much as I was devastated to be part of such a sick plot, I was glad we had an excuse to get our money, and move as far away from those strange people as possible. When my husband finally worked up the courage to ask for our money, "Reza" denied ever promising to give our money back. He said that he had only promised to feed us and put a roof over our heads for a few days and he had fulfilled that promise. It was shocking to me to sit there and listen to such lies. Regardless, I told my husband that we should leave that day and rent a motel with the bit of money we had left. He could then come back later on and try again. He finally agreed. We now only had enough money to afford a very cheap motel and simple food for a few days as my husband still did not have a job. We looked around the town and asked for the cheapest place we could stay in and we finally found one. The motel smelled of cigarettes and alcohol. Hallways smelled of urine. We must have been in a really bad neighbourhood. Those who stayed in that motel looked like drug dealers. Most of them were always drunk. As soon as a woman passed by them, they would stare at her as though they were undressing her in their minds. There was no bathroom in our room. If I wanted to go to bathroom, I had to wait for my husband to accompany me. I was afraid to leave the room on my own. The air quality in that motel was so bad that my baby's eyes were red and watery most of the time and he coughed non-stop each time we left our room.

Thankfully, within the next couple of days, my husband found a job at a construction site. He was being paid hourly so he tried to work as many as 8 or 9 hours a day. The pay was sufficient enough to allow us to lead a simple life and take care of our absolute basic needs. Sometimes my husband would take on a part time job, in the evenings or on odd weekends in restaurants, to earn extra money. The extra money would allow us to live a bit more comfortably. A few days into his first job he found a Persian friend who informed my husband about a very nice motel right across from a beach with an affordable price. He mentioned to my husband that most of the occupants were Persians who had come to Greece to find a way, legally or illegally, to get to North America or Europe. My husband and I were really excited to have found a new place. Within a week we were able to leave that scary motel and move into a really clean and nice place, full of people, most of whom became our friends later on.

Chapter 14 -
In Greece for 27 months:

"It is not the experience of today that drives men mad...it is the remorse for something that happened yesterday, and the dread of what tomorrow may disclose!!! " (Jones Burdette)

****

I have both pleasant and unpleasant memories of our time in Greece. Regardless of how great the people were, and how beautiful Athens was, I missed my baby sister, my family, my friends and my country. No knowing the language, and our less than great financial situation were additional stressors for me. Being responsible for an 18-month old baby, who had not asked for any of this, in a foreign place, was probably the biggest reason why I was depressed all the time. The only bright side was that most people in Athens, especially the younger generation, could speak English. And since I still remembered the very little English I had learned in school years ago, I was somewhat able to communicate with people when the occasion arose. Learning to speak Greek was a challenge for us. I did not feel motivated to learn the language. I found it very difficult. And I did not feel it was too important since I thought that we'd only live there a short time. I was a stay at home mom so I did not need to interact with people that much. At home, Siavash and I watched TV all day long, but since we only viewed channels that offered English programs, we were not exposed to the Greek language either. Mostly though, we watched MTV channels. Siavash absolutely loved music and he would sing and dance all day long while watching the music videos. My husband had a different excuse. In his line of work he did not need to know much Greek. A bit of English combined with a few Greek words took care of his needs all day, but the Greeks were very friendly and would find a way to communicate with us. They gestured with their hands to help us understand them better. When I took Siavash to a playground at a park near where we lived, I was always greeted by older men and women who had brought their grandchildren to the park. They would start with conversing about the weather and most times end up offering suggestions on how to best care for my baby, as they could tell that I was young and inexperienced. I was grateful, for it reminded me of home and how my family and friends genuinely cared for us.

In the motel, I found a few friends whose children were only a couple of years older then Siavash. While they kept me company, their children were great playmates for him. So I felt a bit of relief from the guilt for taking Siavash away from his extended family since he was no longer as lonely. Slowly but surely we had come to accept our situation and adjusted to our new surroundings.

Athens was a beautiful city. People were friendly and the weather was wonderful. Like most large cities, there were more opportunities for people to find decent jobs. I had been born and raised in a big city, Tehran, and could not imagine myself living in a small town, but ironically I connected better with those who had originally come from a small town. I found them to be transparent, warm and more genuine in so many ways. Perhaps I was attracted to the big cities' sophistication and small towns' warmth. Athens offered all of that as most people who lived in Athens were originally from small towns. Athens archaeological and historical sites and museums drew thousands of tourists in every year. Some of the most popular tourists attractions were, Corinth Canal, Archaeological site and theatre at Epidaurus, Archaeological site at Mycenae, Archaeological site and museum at Olympia , Archaeological site and museum at Delphi, the ancient Acropolis, Ancient Agora, Plaka and Monstiraki monuments. It was interesting to find out that while Greece was an agricultural country, the tourism industry contributed the most to its economy. Living in Athens and visiting some of the historical sites, I could understand why they drew in so many tourists each year.

For us though, while historical and archaeological sites were attractive, we were more concerned about our current situation. Our first priority was to visit the United Nations office to present our case and the reason why we had entered Greece illegally. Our new friends and acquaintances helped get us registered with the UN. They had gone through the process and gave us some idea what to expect. To get our case accepted by the UN would mean our entry and stay in Greece would now be considered legal. We could live and work until one of the countries to which we applied for immigration accepted us. However, we only wanted to immigrate to Canada. We were under additional stress since the process to immigrate to North America seemed a bit more difficult, but two of my brothers had already immigrated there so I really hoped to be reunited with them.

At our very first visit to the UN, we were able to look after some preliminary requirement, such as filling out request forms, taking our photos, and providing the address and phone number of the place we were residing at. Next, we had to ensure our names would go on the applicants' list for an interview with a UN official. Due to the number of applicants waiting to be interviewed, we had to wait a few months before we could get in. However, we were told that while we waited for our interview, we would be given a temporary permit to stay in Greece. This news gave us peace of mind. It took us few visits to take care of all the necessary arrangements. Now, we could do nothing more but to wait to receive a letter from the UN with the date and time of our interview.

I was the one who worried the most in our family. To keep my sanity, I tried focusing on one issue at a time, and I chose the most important one which was preparing for our best case to the UN for our interview. I knew we had to pass that hurdle before we could even think about choosing the country to immigrate to. While I was busy looking after Siavash and my homework for the UN, my husband was busy with his work to provide for us.

Siavash was happy and healthy. He was adjusting well to our new living arrangements. Watching my precious baby grow up in a reasonably clean, safe and comfortable place, surrounded by good people, brought so much joy to my life. He meant the world to me. When he was happy and healthy, I was at peace, regardless of our stressful circumstances. By the same token, since so early in life I had lost those that I loved the most, I became an over protective mother. I lived with constant fear something bad might happen in my life. Since he was the only one thing that had gone right, I was afraid to let him out of my sight. Perhaps such intense fear was the reason I felt sad all the time. I also believe that I was giving myself permission to feel my inner turmoil. Now that our life was not in any immediate danger, I no longer wanted to be the strong one and was allowing my emotions to emerge. I felt lonely and lost; helpless and hopeless; and most of all, guilty. I often cried for no reason. No matter how much I tried to hide my tears from Siavash, he often saw me crying, and when I cried, his eyes teared up as well. As a mother, the pain of seeing the confused and sad look of my innocent baby was just too much to bear. I felt responsible for bringing him into this world and then putting him through so much hardship. Slowly, I was slipping into a deep depression I was afraid I could never recover from.

But life was moving on. Days turned into weeks, and weeks into months, before we heard from the UN. We received the letter indicating the date and time of our interview. We were asked to bring in specific documents. We were both excited and anxious at the same time, since there was so much at risk. If we did not pass the interview, they could decide to send us back to Iran. That meant going back to prison and losing Siavash. Thankfully, we had a lot of support from our new friends who now knew our life story. They were constantly on my case to think positively. The day finally arrived when my husband, my baby and I took the bus and, arrived at the UN for our interview. We had a Persian translator waiting for us in the interview room. She was a petite lady with a kind and welcoming face. She was fluent both in English and French. She was very empathetic and did her best to get the UN officials to see our side of the story. I noticed how our interviewers responded to her as she was very capable of articulating what we had to say. When there were no more questions and nothing else we wanted to add, we were told our session had come to an end. We were informed that the verdict would be mailed to us within several weeks. There was no need for us to call and ask for updates. All we had to do, we were told, was to go on as usual and wait to hear from them. During those distressing few months while we waited for the verdict, life was even more chaotic for me. My husband was too busy working, but I had plenty of time to worry about what would happen if we were rejected! I am not sure how I kept my sanity until the day that we finally received the letter. I remember being afraid to open it, fearing it might be bad news. Finally, when my husband got home, I found the courage to open the letter and find that we were granted asylum! That meant we no longer had to worry about extradition in any way. This was the most wonderful news we had in quite a while and it breathed much hope and optimism into our uncertain life. But we were not done yet. Now we needed to find out how long it would take for the Canadian government to respond to our request for immigration. No one could guarantee a time frame in which a certain country would respond. It could take months or years and there was no way to speed up the process in any way. So far we had stayed in Greece for 7 months. We started counting the days until we heard something from Canada. I was in touch with my brothers in Canada often. We always bounced ideas by each other to find a way to get us there faster. We had exhausted all of the possible options until my younger brother came up with the idea of sponsoring us. We were not totally aware of how much my brother had to sacrifice to make this dream a reality. We were just excited to hear that he might be able to help us. My brother was a student at that time but to be qualified as a sponsor, he had to put his schooling on hold and get a job. Since his salary was not too high, he needed additional help. He decided to visit a few churches, explain our situation and ask for help in sponsoring us to Canada. His selfless act paid off and he was able to co-sponsor us to Canada. The whole process, after we were granted immunity from the UN to the time that Canada accepted our immigration request took about 20 months. Words cannot describe how we felt when we were finally notified that our documents were ready and that we could leave for Canada anytime. Now all we had to do was to figure out how to pay for our airfare! Though my husband had worked during the past 27 months, we had no savings. I did not want to ask my brothers for a loan since I knew they were not in a position to help us out financially. If we could not find anyone to loan us the money, we had to stay in Greece until my husband could work and we could save some money. It was difficult though, since what he earned, we had to spend on our basic needs, like food, rent, clothing and transportation. The situation looked so hopeless; I decided to contact my aunt who lived in the States. I knew she would help us somehow even if she had to borrow the money and pay high interest out of her own pocket. Not surprisingly, when I called her to ask for the money, she quickly asked for our bank account information so she could wire the money as soon as possible. The money was in our account within a few days. The last step for us was to sell or donate some of our stuff and do some last minute shopping for our trip to Canada. We had been warned about Canada's cold weather so we wanted to buy clothes appropriate for such a climate. Everything fell into place in a short time. We had booked our flights; completed our shopping adventure and gave away or sold our stuff. The only thing that our friends thought we should do before we left was to go sightseeing! Though we had stayed in Greece for 27 months, we only had a chance to visit few of the most popular tourists' attractions. A good friend of ours offered to be our tour guide and promised to take us to as many places as possible. As I thought about our new journey to yet another strange land I felt overwhelmed and not at all in a mood for sightseeing, but our friend did not take no for an answer. We finally got to visit quite a few rare and remarkable historical sites. And I am glad he was so persuasive. I have fond memories of our time with our friends and pictures that bring back wonderful memories of our time in Greece.

Now we were all set for our trip. As excited as I was to travel to Canada, I was apprehensive to leave all that I had come to know and love. I loved Greece and its warm and friendly people. We had quite a few good friends; I had learned the language to the point that I could communicate with people comfortably. The weather was just amazing and Iran did not feel too far away. So while I was ecstatic that we had finally found a place we could call home, I felt sad at the same time. It was as if I was leaving Iran again and the painful memories of that time were resurfacing. Memories that I tried to bury deep inside me awoke and took over my body and soul. The one thing that kept me going was the hope of a bright future for Siavash so he could grow up and become a successful and happy young man someday. So with a heavy heart and tearful eyes I said goodbye to Greece!

Chapter 15 -
In Canada:

*"Life is not about waiting for the storms to pass....
it's about learning how to dance in the rain."*
(Unknown Source)

****

Finally on September 11th 1990 we arrived in Canada. My younger brother, our sponsor, lived in Edmonton at that time so we flew there first. We had plans to fly to Toronto later on. We had been advised Toronto would be more appropriate for us to build a home. Many Iranians lived in Toronto; the weather was milder than Edmonton; there were more job opportunities; my older brother lived there; and my younger brother was planning to move to Toronto at some point too. However, we needed to take care of our immigration papers in Edmonton so we planned to stay on until all that was handled. Considering the duration of our flight to Edmonton, and our changeover in Frankfurt, we were exhausted. We were anxious and excited as well to find out how our lives would unfold from that point onwards.

We were greeted by my brother at the airport. We were then led to the immigration office to start filling out the necessary paperwork before we entered the city. My brother took care of our baby. He helped us with the forms and with translations where we had trouble on our own. Since Siavash was being entertained, we finished with all that was required of us in couple of hours, and were now ready to leave the airport and officially enter Canada as immigrants.

I immediately fell in love with Edmonton's blue sky, fresh air and clean streets. People were friendly and they had big smiles as they greeted each other on the streets. We finally got to my brother's place where we were able to rest and change into something a bit more comfortable. Siavash was happiest of all as he was able to roam around and inspect his uncle's place. It was wonderful to see him that happy and content and his uncle was doing a great job of spoiling him as much as possible.

During our two- week stay, we got to visit a few tourist attractions, the most among which I was pretty impressed by West Edmonton Mall. Before travelling to Toronto however, we had decided to visit one of our best friends who were now living in Vancouver. We were pretty excited to visit them since they were among people we had met in Greece and had become pretty close with. Siavash looked sad when it was time to say goodbye to his uncle. I was sad too but I had a feeling that we would be reunited soon. Regardless of how we felt, we knew it was time for us to move yet again. We packed our bags and took the bus to Vancouver. I was apprehensive about the long bus ride but Siavash was an angel again and did pretty well throughout our journey. The scenery was just so beautiful that we hardly noticed how many hours it took for us to get there. Vancouver was truly beautiful and very different from Edmonton. The sky in Vancouver was not as blue and as clear as Edmonton, and the sun came out, briefly, only once in a while, but the scenery was absolutely breathtaking. When we arrived, our good friend and his two sons were waiting for us at the bus stop. After a warm greeting we headed home. Our friend's wife was excited to see us, too, and the kids were happy to have a playmate as well. Our reunion under much better circumstances was very pleasant for all of us and we spent a lot of time sharing our memories of our time in Athens together. We had planned to stay there for a week, but we ended up staying two. Our friends were trying to convince us to stay in Vancouver, but since they knew we wanted to join my family in Toronto they did not insist too much. During our two-week stay we got to see few of our other friends we had met in Athens and visited the most popular tourists' attractions as well. Though I liked Vancouver and enjoyed spending time with our friends, I had a feeling that this was not the place I would want to build my home in.

Two weeks passed pretty quickly and it was time for us to say goodbye again and move to a city that was hopefully our last stop. Once in Toronto, we were greeted by my older brother and his friend at the airport. They helped us with our bags and drove us home, where my brother and his friend lived. In order to accommodate us, my brother's friend had just moved out to give us our own room in their two bedroom apartment. Siavash was happy to meet yet another uncle who paid a lot of attention to him. My brother had taken couple of days off work to help us look after some necessary items, among those finding a day care for Siavash and finding a school for us to take ESL courses. We discussed our living arrangements and came to an agreement to live in that apartment for few months together. When my younger brother moved to Toronto, we could rent a bigger place where we could all live together for a while. This way, we had enough time to get on our own feet and decide what we wanted to do with our lives. We were grateful for such an opportunity and for the help and guidance that my brothers were offering until we got used to living in Canada and learned how to best fit in. In about three months, my younger brother was able to leave Edmonton for good and move in to Toronto. We found a nice three bedroom apartment to move to which was not too far from the adult school where my husband and I had registered for our ESL classes. And our place was not too far from Siavash's school when he started attending junior kindergarten.

I was excited to go back to school and truly enjoyed learning a new language. My husband was not as enthusiastic as I was since he felt no immediate need to learn the language. By then, he had found a part time job. He was working at a pizza store owned and operated by Iranians, so he could not practice his English. I was a full time student, and as always, I was thriving in school. I was taking advantage of every opportunity to learn to communicate better, understand and write in English.

My older brother was working full time trying to save enough to enter college or university. Fortunately my younger brother had started university in Toronto so almost all of us in the household were going to school at the time. He had put his life on hold for us, so now I was very happy to see him walking along his path and putting himself first for a change. I have never forgotten his kindness, but have not yet been able to repay him for all that he has done for us. Though I always wished I could return the favour and do something nice for my brother, I was confident that he helped us out of love and with no expectations at all. While I went to school, I volunteered for some non-for profit organizations as well as tutoring a few students in school to keep myself busy.

We were all on our way to achieving the goals we had set for ourselves. I even applied for university. I was accepted at Ryerson's 4-year Social Work program, but I was put on a waiting list because of the number of applicants applying for that program. I was so excited when I heard that I was accepted, and so sad when I found out I had to wait for the following year. Unfortunately, I took that as a sign that perhaps it was best for me not to enter university. I remembered what happened to me in Iran, and I convinced myself that it was safer not to have what I wanted in life. This way I could never lose it. So I gave up on my dream, and passed on the opportunity to live my dream again.

With each passing day, we were becoming more comfortable with the language and life style in Canada and had begun to expand our horizons and find friends. Our lives became more fulfilling and much more fun. I still had three other siblings I missed very much. One of my sisters lived in Germany, another sister and my youngest sister still lived in Iran. And of course, I missed my father who was living with my stepmother in Iran. During the first year of our stay in Canada, we were fortunate enough to have our older sister who lived in Germany visit us for a couple of months. It was great to visit with her again, but I hoped someday we could get our other sisters who lived in Iran to come to Canada. Other than the sadness for not being with all of my family, especially my younger sister, life in general was comfortable for me. I was not particularly happy in my marriage, but since I did not want to cause heartache for Siavash, I never thought about divorce. Thankfully, Siavash and school kept me content; and I felt at peace and comfortable with my living arrangements at the time.

A couple of years passed before we decided to move into a house. Siavash was growing up and our apartment was no longer big enough for all of us to live together comfortably. We found a nice home and moved in together.

CHAPTER 16 –
ARRIVAL OF OUR SECOND
BABY:

"Beauty is transformation of life through Love!" (Unknown Source)

****

About two years after we moved to our new home, I found out that I was pregnant. I remember the day when I gave Siavash, who was 8 at the time, the news. I was picking him up from school and while we were at the bus stop I told him that he was going to have a brother or a sister in a few months. He asked me if I was joking. When I said no, he gave me a big hug and cried. I cried too but our tears were happy tears. Siavash was beside himself and could not believe what he had just heard. As long as I could remember, perhaps when he was only two, he had asked for a baby brother. He always asked how we could get a new baby. Since he was still a baby himself, I would tell him that we would go buy one someday. So every time we went grocery shopping, he asked if we could pick up a baby, too. I would say that one was not available for sale that day. Now, after six years of wishing, begging and even making up stories in school about how many siblings he had, he could finally relax knowing that his wish had come true. I remember when Siavash was about four, he had told his kindergarten teacher that he had five more siblings at home. Apparently everyone was talking about how many brothers and sisters they had and he did not want to feel left out. When his teacher spoke to me that day she said that I looked too young to have six children. I laughed and assured her that Siavash was an only child.

As soon as I told him about my pregnancy, the news was all over his elementary school. Only he had not told them I was pregnant, but that he already had a baby brother at home. When they asked to see the picture, he took the ultrasound photo with him to show it off to everyone. Seeing how happy he was about my pregnancy was making me very happy too; except I was worried if the baby is a girl, how he would react to her. He had always asked for a baby brother and he was not about to give up on that wish. When we asked what he would do if the baby was a girl, he would quickly respond that we could send her back to God and ask that he gives us a baby boy instead. That was all he thought about, and he was not about to let that go. I was a bit concerned; by the same token, I knew of his gentle and kind nature. I knew he would come around in time if the baby turned out to be a girl.

I had always felt resistant at the thought of having another child. I never felt happy in my marriage, nor did I believe that I was a great mom worthy of raising yet another baby. I had suffered so much so early in life that I did not trust this world to be a safe place for my kids as well, and adding one more baby felt more like committing a sin than anything else at the time. My negative outlook on the world, my feeling of inadequacy as a mother, and my unhappy marriage were all of the reasons I did not want to have another child. So my pregnancy was not planned. Also, my husband had serious health issues at the time. As far as the medical world was concerned there was no possible way, other than a miracle, that I could become pregnant. I only found out three months into my pregnancy so I was as surprised as my doctors. They were baffled at such an unexplainable mystery, but they assured me that now that I was pregnant, there were no health concerns for the baby. I was told that I would have a normal delivery and my baby would be just fine.

The anticipation of the arrival of our new baby, and finding out if it was a boy or a girl, brought about so much joy to our family. Days were turning into weeks and weeks into months and the baby was growing up inside me. My husband's work schedule did not allow him to accompany me to my regular doctor appointments. Instead, Siavash who was only too anxious to find out if the baby was a boy or a girl, gladly accompanied me to each appointment. Finally, one day during one of my regular visits my doctor announced that he was able to tell if the baby was a boy or a girl. Siavash was jumping up and down asking the doctor for the information, but my doctor wanted to keep him in suspense for a bit longer. So he grabbed a small piece of paper, turned away from us and wrote something on it. He then folded the paper neatly and carefully, stapled it together to make sure Siavash could not open it. He then turned to Siavash and said that he could open and read the paper once he got home. The tension and suspense was building too much. Siavash looked really nervous, but he agreed to my doctor's terms. On the bus home he was quiet and clearly nervous as this meant a lot to him; perhaps more than we could comprehend. We finally got home and Siavash ran to his room to get the stapler remover and read the note. When I heard his loud scream I knew the baby was a boy!

Time flew and before long, I completed my full term of pregnancy and it was time for the delivery. Since Siavash was ten pounds, I had given birth to him through a C-section. This was most probably the case for my second baby, so I was scheduled for a C-section as well. I was surrounded by my family and friends at the hospital, but the most anxious and excited person waiting outside of the delivery room was Siavash. Finally at 8:30 am on November 8th I gave birth to a beautiful, healthy baby boy who was ten pounds and two ounces; I named him Afsheen. An extended family member, a man whom I had come to love, respect and trust as my father, suggested that I name the baby Afsheen. I said yes since this was also the name of an Persian warrior. When I came to after couple of hours, the nurses brought my baby to me. As soon as I had him in my arms, Afsheen grabbed my finger and it was right at that moment that I knew I had just fallen in love with him. I cried as I held him close to me and thanked the universe for such a miracle.

But I was also in a lot of physical pain and I cried quietly when I was alone. Since this was my second baby, I already knew about hormonal changes and possible post partum depression that some mothers experienced. I could not stop crying neither when I was alone at the hospital nor when I was discharged and went home. My older sister, who had come to stay with me from Germany for a while to help out had a tough time understanding why I cried so much. I could not share what was eating away at me. It was true that part of my depression was due to my pregnancy, excessive weight I had put on and severe pain as a result of my surgery. However I knew deep down that I cried mostly because I knew I did not want to be married anymore. I could no longer pretend that things, for us as a couple, were working out but I was terrified to share my feelings with anyone in my family.

I was miserable during the time that was supposed to be the happiest time of my life. How could anyone deal with such feelings when so much was at stake? I was devastated, irritated, withdrawn, and depressed. All I could do was to pray that I would find the strength to live through this period while keeping my sanity. I could not contemplate divorce so I decided to do everything in my power to push such thoughts away. I prayed for guidance to find a way to distract myself so I could change my focus; and strangely enough, God answered my prayers by giving me a baby who hardly slept. Afsheen was awake almost all day and night and often cried for no reason at all. To say that he was a handful is an understatement. He was too naughty and fearless for his own good and I had a hard time catching up with him to keep him from any harm. Such distraction proved to be powerful enough to keep me from thinking about my unhappy marriage. So for the time being, I was certain that I did not want to go through with a disruption in my life; or to be responsible for putting my family through such distress and heartache.

Chapter 17 –
Building a Career/
Finding permanent
employment:

"When you are making a success of something, it is not work. It is a way of life. You enjoy yourself because you are making your contribution to the world." (Andrew Granatelli)

****

Four years had passed and I had become even more miserable, emotionally, mentally and physically. Financially, we were not in a good shape either. I knew it was time for me to make some changes and perhaps turn my life around. Afsheen was now four. I felt the first step for me was to find a full time job. I had a feeling that I needed to become financially independent sooner rather than later. My search for an affordable business training institute paid off really quickly. I had heard of a learning centre that offered a variety of business courses to get people prepared for clerical and office positions. They offered computer courses, as well as communication and hands on business etiquette courses. This was exactly what I was looking for. I quickly enrolled myself in an office administration certificate program. As we could not afford to put Afsheen in a day care yet, I started by taking evening and weekend classes. This way I was home during the day to look after him. For the evenings and weekends, I had to rely on my husband. Luckily my best friend Zahra, who lived close to me, offered to help take care of Afsheen on days when my husband had to work late. I had about an hour's drive to school so I had to leave the house in a timely manner. As challenging as it was to plan everything and get myself to school everyday, I was able to attend school on time and on a regular basis. I was happy that I was out of the house and learning something new that could help me find a full time job. I was well motivated to take as many classes as possible. My goal was to fulfill all of the requirements and obtain my certificate ahead of schedule. Since I already had taken typing as part of my ESL courses, I had one less thing to worry about. Plus my typing skills enabled me to get my assignments done in a timely manner as well.

As a result of all of my hard work and Zahra's help with Afsheen, I was done in three months instead of the projected six months completion period. After obtaining my certificate and gaining knowledge of the most popular office applications, I finally worked up the courage to create a resume. I knew that I would be targeting an entry level clerical/office position until I could figure out what I really wanted to do. While in school I had heard of agencies that helped people find temporary employment. I started making appointments with as many temp agencies as I could to increase my chances of finding employment as soon as possible. To get accepted by a temp agency, I had to go through quite a few interviews and pass many tests. So for the next couple of months when my school was done, I spent a lot of time scheduling tests and interviews. I finally registered with four large temp companies specialized in office work. Within a month of my registration I had offers for short term employment opportunities. I had to turn down a few work assignments since the locations were too far from my house, but luckily I was able to find a few that were convenient for me to get to.

I still remember how anxious I was when I accepted my first assignment. I was temporarily replacing a lady who had been in a car accident and had to stay home for two weeks. Working for that company was a wonderful learning experience for me; one that boosted my confidence level and kept me going. When I was done, my employers provided such great feedback to my temp agency that they kept calling me for more assignments. I now had more hope that one day soon I would be able to find permanent employment.

My second assignment led me to the third assignment at an IT company. My third assignment became my first fulltime permanent job in Canada! It took me two and half years from the day I registered with temp agencies to finally secure a full time position. I truly believe that the knowledge and experience gained in my previous job in Iran along with all that I learned after my escape from Iran, was absolutely necessary to get me where I wanted to go in life.

Though doing office work was far from what I had envisioned for me in life, I was grateful for the opportunity to be financially independent especially at that point. I started to work with amazing people, many of whom became close personal friends later on. I felt tremendously supported and appreciated by my team and felt that I was contributing to building a robust team. As I grew more, I blossomed and became much happier and more content once again. In my position, as an administrative assistant, I had to multi task, think on my feet most of the time, work with minimal supervision and communicate with other departments, as well as clients on a regular basis. I was never tired or bored even when I had to put in long hours because I felt I was making a difference. The busier I became the more I pushed myself to learn all that I could. As a result, I kept taking on more work. I was eager to start each day in anticipation of new learning opportunities. At the end of each week, I was able to look back and take pride in my accomplishments, which in turn encouraged me to do more.

I worked with some remarkable managers who were natural born leaders; among those I would like to acknowledge and thank my boss, Perry, for his unconditional support and guidance. Perry believed in me and always treated me as I could be, not as I was; he inspired me to become more. He saw my potential and always took time to acknowledge my efforts every step of the way. This in turn encouraged me to examine my options, think for myself and take initiative. And since I was treated with the utmost respect and appreciation, I felt comfortable to offer my opinion when the occasion called for it. Through Perry's encouragement and the financial support of my company, I was able to enrol at a community college and obtain my designation with honours in the field of office administration. My full time work schedule, along with the part time schooling and my 24/7 job taking care of my kids and my household was admittedly exhausting. By the same token, I found it rewarding. In so many ways I felt more confident and content. I finished my certificate in three years, instead of four, and then spent two additional years studying different subjects. I took communication courses, writing for business, sales and marketing, psychology, human resources and human behaviour courses. All of the courses were quite relevant to my work and useful for my professional and personal life. My efforts did not go unnoticed. In a few short years I was promoted and able to enjoy better financial rewards there after.

Eventually many of my colleagues and managers moved on and our paths never crossed again. Yet the effects of their mentoring and guidance stayed with me long after they were gone. It was as though they had left blueprints for me to follow so I knew I would not get lost on my path. Without a doubt those people played an important role in shaping one of the most significant chapters of my life. Being exposed to insights and perspectives of such exceptional people helped me learn valuable lessons and apply them to my professional and personal life. It opened up my mind and my heart to new possibilities and provided me with opportunities to learn more about myself as well.

While my professional life was unfolding wonderfully before me, I still had to face challenges in my personal life which were wearing me out. The time had come for me to look inward and face my fears. I needed to find out why I was not at peace; why I was not experiencing personal happiness; why I felt inadequate; why I felt like a failure. Facing my own demons and admitting that I was not perfect was the most challenging task for me. I now knew why so very few people were willing to look inside instead of blaming the world for their misfortunes. It was much easier to say that this was all done to me rather than admitting I had a big part in most of them. In someway, perhaps I had allowed some of the unpleasant events to happen and keep happening to me. As I found the courage to finally travel through the less travelled roads, I became more apprehensive and fearful, but I knew I could not turn back now. I knew too much by then to want to continue living a miserable life there after. It was as though I had to step into the darkness to find the light I so longed for. Yes I was terrified; I was lonely; I did not have much support; but I was determined to turn my life around and so I did!

CHAPTER 18 -
THE BREAK UP OF MY
FAMILY...MY DIVORCE:

"Things don't go wrong and break your heart so you can become bitter and give up. They happen to break you down and build you up so you can be all you were intended to be." (Charlie "Tremendous" Jones)

****

I don't remember a time when I ever felt happy or content in my marriage. The truth is that two weeks prior to our wedding day, I had changed my mind. My husband was the only one who knew about this but he did not want us to back out. He thought that I was stressed out and overwhelmed, but I knew it was more than that. But he persisted and I finally gave in. I thought of the embarrassment I would cause my family if I changed my mind so close to the wedding. So I decided to go through with it, regardless of how I truly felt. I could not see any other option available to me. I promised myself that I would make this marriage work no matter what. I did not have the emotional strength I needed to face my family or our society's rejection, so I kept quiet. I was too young and naive to imagine how unimaginably difficult it could be to start a new life knowing that my partner and I did not belong together. We were not in love, at least not according to my translation of love, and I could sense that we were just too different in very many ways, but I got married when I was almost 20 years old. Throughout the seventeen years of my marriage, I never felt appreciated, loved, cared for, heard, understood or important in anyway. In all fairness, I don't believe I was able to extend all that I so longed for to my husband either. In the back of my mind, while I never contemplated divorce at least during the first several years, I always knew I would not be growing old with my husband. Instead of dealing with my feelings, I decided to bury them deep inside and pretend that all was well.

I am a firm believer that things always happen when the time is absolutely right. So when we moved to Canada and when I finished school and obtained a full time job I felt it was time to focus on my persona life. Unfortunately that meant the break up of my marriage. I had always been independent and able to stand on my own feet; so I knew I could handle taking care of my children on my own. Now that I had the financial means to support my family as well I was convinced, more than ever, that I should break free and end this loveless marriage. While I was positively convinced that divorce was the only possible option for me, I felt absolutely devastated at the thought of putting my children through such distress. By the same token, I knew I could no longer go on pretending that all was well when that was furthest from the truth. I came up with the idea of living under the same roof with my husband not as a couple but as roommates. So without sharing my decision with anyone except with my husband, I started yet another painful chapter of my life. He responded with indifference and coldness that he was okay with this too. He did not try to change my mind or encourage me to re-think my decision. I was not surprised since I could sense that he did not have strong feelings for me either. My intention ultimately was to protect my children anyway I could even if that meant sacrificing my own physical, mental and emotional well being. During those three long years of my life living with him as roommates, I buried myself in piles of extra work at the office so to help ease the pain of living a lie. As a result of putting myself through such distress, my health began to decline and I felt sick most of the time. With each passing day, I found it more difficult to come home to my children; so I wondered if my decision to stay in the marriage had actually defeated the very purpose I was putting up with such challenges. Despite my efforts to keep what was really going on from my children, I had a feeling that they sensed something was wrong. The negative energy in our house surely affected them more than I could realize at that point. Finally, after enduring three years of agonizing pain, and after seeing a few therapists to get help, I called it quits! My husband was not surprised since we he had many conversations when I had threatened to leave him. He did not take me seriously at the time, but to my husband's disbelief, I stood by my decision this time and insisted on a divorce as I could no longer continue on with this lie. I had finally found the courage to open up to my kids and my family and despite extremely difficult obstacles, I finally filed and eventually finalized my divorce at the age of 37. I felt a considerable amount of guilt because of my children, but I felt justified in wanting a divorce. In my heart I knew that I had done everything in my power not to break up this family but I saw no other option at the time. Needless to say that my family's reactions was worst than I had imagined; and my kids were absolutely devastated when they found out we were getting a divorce. Though I was determined to keep strong and stand by my decision, I was not sure how I would keep my sanity and survive the guilt and shame I felt every time I looked at my kids. In my heart, I knew without a doubt, that this was the right choice.

It took all of us as a family, my two sons and I, several years to come to terms with this break up. Despite all the suffering I had to endure, somewhere inside of me I felt a quiet space of peacefulness that promised all would be well soon, and that was exactly what happened. We were taking things one day at a time and dealing with issues as they came up; and soon something incredible started to happen. I started to appreciate and enjoy my kids a lot more. My world became a happier place and I felt more alive and energetic than I could ever remember during my married life. I slowly began to realize that I could get to a place where I could be a great parent regardless of my imperfections and shortcomings. I began to see that I did not need to sacrifice my own happiness to make my kids happy. In fact, I realized that I needed to be happy and content to help create a happy family. I slowly began to feel less angry and more understanding and forgiving of myself and others. I was in a better physical and emotional shape that I had been in years. I excelled at work and felt happier in my social life too. Eventually my friends and family started to notice such changes in me and they were truly happy for me. Most importantly my kids and I became closer and that was the biggest gift I could ever ask for. As a natural progression of my journey I got to learn amazing lessons that I would never have learned had it not been for such painful experiences. I learned how to be independent and in charge of all aspects of my life as well as giving less importance to what others thought I should be, do, or have. I learned that I can take responsibility for my life without a need to blame myself or anyone else for anything that had gone wrong in my life. I learned not to live my life according to my parents, family or friends' vision any longer. Instead I learned that it was okay for me to follow my passion and live my life the way I had envisioned it for myself. I realized I was the only one who had held me back in life for all those years and I vowed not to let that happen again. The more I started taking care of myself, the more I cherished my kids and so we became closer than ever. My mission was to lead by example and become a positive role model for my kids. I wanted them to see me as a confident, strong, independent and determined woman with goals and aspirations. With all that in mind, my intention was to focus on how to move forward and what could go right in our lives. I learned that cultural and social indoctrinations and negative experiences early in life could inadvertently shape our outlook of life. However, I also learned that what ultimately determines our level of happiness is our openness to view life through different vantage points. I learned that there are things in life I have no control over, but I always have the freedom, despite extremely difficult circumstances, to react to those events anyway I choose to.

Looking back at that chapter of my life, I can say with utmost conviction that I have never regretted my decision to end my marriage. However, I have always regretted putting two innocent children through so much anguish and heartache. This has been an ongoing challenge for me in life. Though I feel better than I used to, I still have not fully forgiven myself for the pain and discomfort I had caused my children, but I am working on it.

Chapter 19 -
My personal
development journey –
Becoming a Life Coach

"Learning is finding out what you already know.
Doing is demonstrating that you know it. Teaching
is reminding others that they know it just as well
as you do. We are all learners, doers and teachers."
(Richard Bach)

****

My journey started when I was too young to understand or articulate my thoughts and feelings; long before I could comprehend what life was all about. When I was in grade one I remember asking my classmates if they knew how we could meet God. I was curious about how the universe was being run and why our world was the way it was. Though exploring such questions was fascinating to me, at such young age, those thoughts made me apprehensive. I felt mature beyond my years and that was the cause of my loneliness and overwhelmed feeling. I was different from most kids my age and that made me feel self-conscious and uncomfortable in my own skin. But I was not always sad. At times I felt unexplainable joy deep inside perhaps because I had envisioned who I wanted to become when I grew up. I knew where I wanted to go but I did not know how extremely challenging it could be to get on that path and stay on it! I knew I would be working as a teacher, a guide, a coach or a mentor. Perhaps my gift was sensing people's pain as though I was feeling it myself. I understood, intuitively, that people's suffering could largely be attributed to how they viewed the world. I could see that most people felt obligated to live their lives according to what their family, society or culture deemed proper.

I have talked about my love for school, books and learning frequently throughout this book; perhaps it is time now to talk about why I gave up on all that for almost two decades.

After going throughout extremely painful circumstances so early in life, I convinced myself that all of my heartaches had emanated from my curiosity for life; my thirst to learn and examine different views; and for standing up for my beliefs. Consequently, I decided to choose a completely different path in life. I chose a path of denial. I decided to compromise on what I really wanted in life. Something deep inside was eating away at me but I chose not to face it. I felt that I did not have the courage to deal with it. Instead, I tried running away from it. As a result, I lived with bitter disappointment that prevented me from ever experiencing true happiness. I could no longer recognize myself; and I most certainly did not like myself.

The journey of hopelessness had started right after I was captured, at 16, and thankfully came to a slow but steady end after my divorce. Perhaps it is true that sometimes the most heartbreaking events in life can force us to re-evaluate our priorities and look for a fresh start. At 37, it seemed as though I had been given a second chance in life. For the first time in a long time I felt alive again. Slowly but surely I started to feel the passion I once felt for life and all that it had to offer. Once again I found myself drawn to books so to satisfy my unquenchable thirst for learning. I was excited for the opportunity to learn all that I could about me. I wanted to find out why my life had turned out the way it did. I intuitively knew to change my life for the better, I needed to change from the inside out. Through difficult lessons early in life, I had learned that my happiness did not depend on external circumstances, the world or other people's approval of me. I also realized that I needed a lot of support to get myself out of the vicious cycle that had been running my life for decades.

When I became fully aware of the causes for my unhappiness, I decided to take actions to change my direction in life. For starters, I committed to weekly counselling sessions so to find the right support in helping me delve deep inside myself. I attended live personal development seminars, took advantage of books, CD's and audio tapes by well known authors in that field, and socialized with people who had gone through similar experiences in life and came out of it with much success.

Though I had taken some steps towards my goals on my own, one of my close friends, "Sam" was in fact the catalyst in helping me get my life back in order. Thanks to his support and persuasion, I got back to the personal development journey that had started when I was six. "Sam" and I worked together, and since we had a similar outlook on life, we quickly became friends. One day he approached me to ask if I wanted to accompany him to a complimentary personal development seminar that evening. I asked what it was about and he said that I needed to experience it for myself as it was not something he could describe to me. I wondered why he thought that seminar would be useful to me so I asked him about it. He asked that I trust him and just go with him. Perhaps he could see something was eating away at me so much so that my well groomed and put together exterior could not fool him. He talked some more about the seminar and soon I had tears in my eyes. The pain of what was buried inside me was resurfacing and that was just too unbearable for me. I almost wanted to run away from him, but a powerful force inside me encouraged me to go with him; so I said yes. I stayed and listened to him some more as he briefly shared his personal story. He talked about his life altering experiences which he never thought possible before he enrolled on that program. His feeling was that he had been walking with blindfold on all of his life; but now that the blindfold was off, he could finally see clearly what life was all about. I had always trusted "Sam". He had a glow on his face as he spoke that gave me hope. He seemed much gentler, more patient and more at peace. It seemed as though he was viewing the world differently and that was the source of his new found inner bliss! I longed for all that myself.

"Sam" and I talked to two of our other close friends and got them to agree to come along as well. I remember that night quite well. We always had fun when the four of us got together but that night was extra special. We had dinner that night before driving to the location where they were holding the free seminar. Apparently current and previous students would bring along their families and friends to such sessions. As we entered the building we were greeted by cheerful staff welcoming us in. The session started with a key note by one of the course leaders. She formally welcomed the students, their families and friends and then moved on giving details about the courses offered. She invited the graduates to share their experiences and talk about their perspective on life in general before, and after, their enrolment. I must admit that I was overwhelmed by hearing such powerful stories that hit so close to home for me.

As we listened to people talking in a large auditorium that night, we found out more what the seminar was all about.

When the seminar was over, the staff and volunteers made themselves available to answer questions. Ultimately, they were hoping to enthuse and encourage those who were considering enrolling in some courses to take action and register that night. Those who had decided to register right away were quickly looked after. Those who had not made up their minds were encouraged to share their concerns. Most people who wished to discuss further the idea of joining in were accommodated by staff in one-on-one meetings at the center. I was among those who did not need to be convinced, but I only had one issue that concerned me. I thought the courses were too expensive for my budget. Since I was a single parent and on a fixed income, I did not think I could afford to spend that much money on a course. It did not take me too long to convince myself that one course would not be too much of a financial burden. I enrolled myself that night. Immediately after, I felt relieved, excited and apprehensive at the same time. Making such a spontaneous decision was not difficult after seeing a sneak preview of what the course could ultimately do for me. My anxiety came from the resistance about revisiting my hidden scars and perhaps sharing them with others. I thought I had gone completely mad to want to put myself through such an intense experience. The course was to start in a few weeks. I was concerned that my fearful thoughts might convince me to back off. Thankfully I decided to go through with it. What happened after that changed my life forever and for the better.

The most anticipated day finally arrived. As I walked in to our class, I immediately felt intimidated by seeing that many people in the room. Despite the fact that I appeared to be an extravert, I was a shy person who normally did not initiate a conversation in social gatherings. So I chose a spot somewhere in the front of the room and quickly sat down instead of walking around and socializing with others. People from all walks of life were in attendance. There were pilots, engineers, house wives, sales executives, teachers, office workers, artists, mechanics, business owners, students, coaches and nurses to name some. We had different age groups in the room; some were in their twenties; some in their thirties, forties, fifties and we had some who were seventy or older. Participants came from different financial, marital and social status. Some had come a long way from home to participate at this seminar, and were staying at hotels close by for the duration of the course. Being exposed to such diversity provided an excellent learning opportunity for me. All I had to do was to listen without judgment and with an open mind.

Our facilitator welcomed the students and went over ground rules for the duration of the course. As she started talking, I noticed that I had gotten busy looking to find something wrong with her. My first impression of the facilitator was that she was cold and bossy. The fact was that there was nothing wrong with the way she communicated. I was trying to find something I could use to dismiss her in my mind. Fear of opening up and exposing my wounds and scars was powerful. I felt that by dismissing her in that way, I did not have to acknowledge a heavy burden I had been carrying on my fragile shoulders. What she was saying actually made sense and indeed applied to me more than I cared to admit. I noticed my resistance and the reasons for it so I decided, despite my inner turmoil, to stick around a bit longer. The pain seemed too unbearable at times but something kept me in that seat and forced me to deal with it once and for all. I could feel the heavy weight on my chest preventing me from breathing with ease. I had a hard time pulling myself together. Something strange was happening to me. The more upset and out of control I felt, the more I became determined to stay for the entire course; and that was without a doubt one of the best decisions I had made in my life up to that point.

Our instructor had planned a day full of different activities; she used different themes to get her message across and it was working beautifully. There was no room for boredom. On the contrary people were kept well focused and interested as a result of using such versatility. There were always topics for group discussions; then she would call upon people to share their experiences around some of those topics. The instructor would work with those people one on one, in front of the class, so others would observe and learn from it as well. She then would provide opportunities for feedbacks or questions.

"Sam" had promised me a transformational experience. He was convinced that I would take something valuable out of it if I keep an open mind. I believe he was talking about some kind of breakthrough. While I tried not to keep my hopes up, I did my best to follow through and work on our assignments with enthusiasm. I put on my listening ears to get as much as possible and took notes as much as possible.

Despite my scepticism, on the second day of our session, something triggered a strange feeling inside me. It was as though a light bulb had gone on in my head! All of a sudden everything made sense to me. For that brief moment, I no longer felt the heavy burden on my shoulders. The pain in my chest was gone and for the first time in a long time I was able to breathe comfortably. I felt like my heart was going to fly off my chest any minute. While I was thrilled about my new discovery, I was disappointed that it had taken that long for me to see such a simple truth. It was devastating to realize that while I was too busy blaming the world for taking my power away from me, it was actually me who had handed it over to them in a platter! It was me who chose to live my life as a victim. It was me who had built a bigger prison inside of me that kept me captive for two decades. After all, the bars that imprisoned me were made of my own mistaken beliefs. It was terrifying to look into the eyes of my worst enemy only to find out that all those years she had been staring back at me with her distressing eyes. I was looking at me! It took me a while to get over the initial shock of my discovery that day and I was shaken for a good part of the day. My prayers for a second chance in life had finally been answered. I suddenly remembered what my friend, "Sam", had told me. Only now I could truly see that he was right! Indeed, I had been walking most of my life with blindfold on.

To this date, such awakening remained one of the most profound and overwhelming experiences in my life.

As the joy and shock of my new discovery about myself was wearing off a bit, I noticed my negative self talk. I was being pulled into blame games again. I interpreted being responsible for my life to "I was to blame for all that had gone wrong in my life." Obviously, I had missed the whole point. I was operating on automatic pilot mode again, unable to accept or forgive myself and move on. Soon the overpowering feeling of fear, guilt, shame, regret, resentment and unworthiness came back; only this time it was much more powerful. It has always been easy for me to forgive others; forgiving myself on the other hand, had always been an impossible mission. Even when I judged others for any reason, I could come up with many excuses why they had behaved the way they did and let it go at some point. Yet, when I caught myself making a mistake, no matter how insignificant it was, I treated myself harshly. I became my own merciless judge, jury and executioner. Now that I look back, I am not surprised of how quickly I turned the joy of my new discovery into more pain and suffering.

I was thinking to myself: "Could it be that I made a mistake by taking this course?" "Would I have been better off to accept the pain I was used to instead of intensifying it in this way?" "Had I not punished myself long enough in the past?" Such questions kept me preoccupied for a while and helped create more chaos and inner turmoil.

Regardless, I did not give up and stayed with the course; and I am so very glad that I did. As the course progressed through rest of the afternoon and evening, I heard that love and forgiveness starts with myself. I was baffled. "Wouldn't that be considered a selfish act to put myself above everyone else?"; I asked myself. After all, My <u>Must Love</u>, <u>Must Accept</u> and <u>Must Forgive</u> list did not include me at all. I was never a priority for me, and I had trained others to treat me the same. Now I was listening that my very freedom and peace of mind depended on putting myself first; in loving myself! I needed to look at myself in the mirror and say I love you! They might have as well asked me to climb Mount Everest! Slowly this so called breakthrough seemed more like heartbreak to me.

This was understandably a difficult concept for me to comprehend, so I eagerly shared my new discoveries with others in my class during our morning and afternoon breaks. I wanted to hear their insights and perspectives hoping to find out that I was not the alone in this journey. While we shared our stories I began to notice a common theme in almost all of our complaints and dissatisfactions. I had a hard time finding someone who had not in one way or other been through similar painful experiences as I had. Of course, I was sad to find out how almost all of us suffered through life; but in a way I felt at peace knowing that I was not that different from those around me after all.

Suddenly I started remembering my time in prison. I recalled how I was able to forgive those who took me away from my mom's dying bed. Then I remembered forgiving my best friend for leading the government agents to me and letting them take me away in front of my mom's tearful eyes. I must admit that it was a whole lot easier to forgive my best friend than to forgive those four agents and the lead prosecutor, especially him, who was in charge that night. I remembered what empowered me to forgive those who had done the unthinkable. I saw them as those who still walked with their blindfold on; those who blindly acted upon their beliefs; and those who never examined the validity of what they held as their truth. I remembered feeling empathetic towards them thinking of them as lost souls. I asked myself how I would behaved if I viewed the world through their eyes; if I held their truth to be the ultimate truth for me; and if had acted more out of fear than love. I truly believe that such contemplations gave me the strength to set myself free at that time. And ironically my very survival in prison was guaranteed the minute I let go of my hatred.

Now almost two decades later, while taking a course, things started to look clearer. I slowly began to comprehend why I had such a difficult time relating to others and why I did not have a descent relationship with myself. I began to understand why I was terrified to be alone with myself. Why Fear? Because I felt lonely; and because I resented the person I was alone with, myself! I was terrified of finding out that I was in fact a BAD person who got what she deserved in life; a bad person who caused her family a tremendous amount of grief; and a bad person who in the end would die like a victim just like she lived as one. I felt exhausted and very emotional. I cried often as I listened to other people's heartbreaking stories. There was a profound sadness inside me. By the same token, hearing other people's horrifying stories made me realize how much I had to be thankful for.

Of so many stories I heard throughout that weekend, one particularly stayed with me and that was about a young girl who was raped when she was a teenager. It was very difficult to listen to her and not cry. After that horrifying incident, she had taken over torturing herself for something she had no control over. She cried as she spoke shamefully. She shared that for all those years she felt like she was a bad seed; she felt dirty, worthless, unlovable, undeserving, and damaged goods. She never worked out the courage to tell anyone about that horrific attack since she thought they would blame her for it. She had come to believe that she had deserved to be brutalized like that and perhaps she had asked for it. We could sense her intense hatred towards herself. It was obvious that she was stuck in that story and unable to move on with her life. She had completely lost faith in herself and could not trust anyone now. As a result, building quality relationships with those around her seemed impossible to her.

As heartbreaking as her story was, it seemed to be the perfect theme for what our course leader intended to teach us that day. She used the story to teach us how to discern the truth from our own made up stories. I was shaking my head thinking that no one would be able to help that girl after all that she had been through. I was thinking that no one could deny the affects of such sadism in her life; and no one could help her move on. What happened next proved me wrong!

The course leader who seemed stern was compassionate towards this girl. She acknowledged the fact that this experience was a horrific one; and that almost all people would feel the same way as she did if they had gone through the same thing. She then asked her to think about what part of her experience was "the fact" – what she believed with absolute conviction and without a doubt and what part of it was "the made up story". The poor girl who had been sobbing nonstop took a deep breath and started to speak again. After she collected her thoughts for a minute, she said that "the fact" was that she was raped; and there was not doubt about that. Then she became silent and waited for the course leader to respond. After a brief pause, the course leader asked the young girl to examine her beliefs about herself after that brutal attack. She was particularly asked to focus on the story about her being a bad seed, dirty, worthless, undeserving, and a damaged goods. While she took her time to reflect on those words, using colourful markers, the course leader put those words on a big whiteboard that faced all of us in the room. There was a powerful silence in the room. We could hear a needle dropping on the floor. The young girl finally broke the silence; she slowly turned around and looked at each one of those words on the board. As I recall, she started off with the word "bad seed". She said that her parents had always said that her careless behaviours one day would get her in trouble, but she had never listened to them. Now she was convinced that they were right about her; and that she was indeed so bad that her own family was ashamed of her. The course leader and people in the room were all quiet. She then went over each word and explained why she thought they were each true about her. When she was done, the course leader asked her another question. Facing her, she asked whether she had gone out that night asking to be raped. The young girl was shocked. She was speechless as she could not believe what she had just been asked. Still crying, she responded with conviction, "of course not". There was an awkward silence in the room again. She was shaking uncontrollably. The course leader gave her few minutes to go through all those emotions; then she calmly walked towards her and asked if she could ask another question. When the girl nodded her head in agreement, she gently asked the young girl to explain why she had convicted herself of a crime that was committed by someone else. The girl, who was crying uncontrollably up to that moment, suddenly stopped and looked at the course leader. Her eyes were shining and her face just lit up. It was as though a heavy weight was lifted off her shoulder all of a sudden. Facing the course leader, she then started speaking in a calm manner. She said that she had no idea how she had come to make up such stories about herself.

With the course leader's help, the young girl began to understand the difference between the fact, "she was raped", and the story, "she was a bad seed and she must have deserved what came to her." I must say that I learned a lot from that experience and I am sure others did as well. Many people walked out to her and gave her a big hug and held her in their arms. While she was sobbing they told her that they never, for a minute, thought of her as being bad in anyway. They told her she was deserving of love just like any other human being. That was one of the most touching experiences during that course. That experience opened my eyes, touched my heart and helped me become more compassionate towards myself and others.

After that day, I was able recall many examples of where I had failed to make such distinctions in my own personal life, and as a result suffered through painful experiences. But now things had changed for me; it was as if a door had opened up where there were only walls before. I felt as though I had just woken up from a terrifying nightmare that took about twenty years. I felt a sense of optimism knowing that my new found discoveries could be the way out of the vicious cycle of guilt, blame, fear, doubt and resentment. I now felt excited to share my new perspectives with everyone and even more so eager to hear their new discoveries. During our lunch or dinner breaks, we would sit at a large table and talk about our stories.

I could not help but remember how I had walked around in pain, for years, feeling as though I was all alone in this world. I remember thinking that the universe had singled me out, and that everyone was out to get me since I was somehow unworthy of true happiness. I felt that life had handed me a raw deal and that I was set up for failure from the moment I was born! Buying into such lies and made up stories, had an adverse affect on all aspects of my life.

After such profound experience, I became determined to find out and face my self-destructive patterns that had made life unbearable for me. It took me years of intensive schooling, studies, counselling, coaching and mentoring to finally begin to recognize those patterns. As a result, I finally found out how and why I was trapped, and learned new ways to look at the world, people and myself. I learned how to set myself free! The dead girl I once thought would never come alive, came back to life!

For the first time in decades I felt glad to be alive and I was truly happy to be me! I now believed that I could be, do and have all that I set my mind to, so I began to focus on my long lost dream. What was my dream? I wanted to work with people as a teacher, a guide, or a coach. I dreamed of reaching out to those who experienced pain and discomfort in their lives. I dreamed of motivating, enthusing and encouraging people to examine the real reasons why they lead unhappy lives for so long. I wanted to help people discover and bring to life the strong yet gentle genius inside them that had been lost for so long. I wanted to remind people that while we have a responsibility towards all human beings on this planet, we have a responsibility towards ourselves too. We are responsible to create the best life for us and to experience happiness and inner peace so to help create a happier world. My long lost dream was not only to hold people's hands but touch their hearts…and so through some extraordinary and miraculous encounters, my dream came true. I found what best suited me along that path. I became a life coach!

I now believe that I have found the true meaning of this quote, by Howard Thurman, and how it applies to me in my life:

"Don't ask yourself what the world needs; ask yourself what makes you come alive, and then go do that; because what the world needs is people who have come alive."

CHAPTER 20 -
LIFE TODAY:

*"Three passions, simple but overwhelmingly strong, have governed my life:
the longing for love, the search for knowledge, and unbearable pity for the
suffering of mankind. These passions, like great winds, have blown me
hither and thither, in a wayward course, over a deep ocean of anguish,
reaching to the very verge of despair..... This has been my life. I have
found it worth living, and would gladly live it again if the chance were
offered me."*
(Bertrand Russell, a philosopher from the 20th century)

****

I am a work in progress! My life is paradoxical yet harmonious. I have
days full of positive anticipation, as well as unpromising and bleak
days. There are days that I feel lonely and days that I feel connected and
whole. Some days I show compassion towards myself, and some days I
am least kind to myself. There are days that I doubt my ability to deal
with what life throws at me, and days that I feel my tremendous inner
strength and resilience. Some days I feel that life has dealt me a raw
deal, and some days I feel most grateful for all of my life experiences,
regardless of how painful they might have been.

Trivial issues still bring me down from time to time; but when I am
bogged down by toxic emotions it does not take me as long to rise above
them. The episodes don't happen as often as they used to; and such

emotions are less intense and have less power over me. I can respond instead of react more often. When I judge myself or others, I can quickly bring myself back and remind myself to be more compassionate and forgiving.

One thing is for certain though - I am no longer a victim! – And I am better than I used to be!

If I were to describe my old state of being, it would look something like this:

The "old Kathy's" response to challenges:

- She took things personally believing the universe was out to get her!
- She blamed people and circumstances for her misery!
- She blamed herself for all that had gone wrong in her life!
- She shut down, resigned, and interpreted her experience as evidence that she did not deserve to be happy! And that she was a bad person deserving of punishment!

The "new Kathy's" response to challenges:

- She allows herself to go through the emotions instead of suppressing them, feel ashamed or guilty because of them!
- She is now in touch with her tremendous inner strength, determined to get up and keep going every time she falls!
- She is able to catch herself just as she is about to blame herself or others. Instead, she redirects her energy to focus on the lessons she could learn from such experiences!
- As she is about to judge herself or others, or when she does judge, she quickly brings herself back by reminding herself that she wants to be free of her ego!
- She now believes that she is deserving of love and happiness just like every other being!
- She no longer feels that she should be perfect to be a good person. She is able to embrace all of her as a whole!
- She is no longer lonely since she now likes the person she is alone with!

- Now in the midst of periodic chaos and disarray in her life, she is able to pause for a moment and say, "this too shall pass!"

I have experienced much trauma in my life some of which, for personal reasons, I left out of this book. Yet, I can not deny the transformational power such experiences have had in my life. Perhaps it is true that the best lessons in life are also the hardest lessons. Personally speaking, the best opportunities for my growth arose out of the most challenging experiences in my life. Living through trauma, forced me to redirect my attention inward to look for answers to my problems. Consequently, I got to know myself better. I learned to be grateful and not take for granted all that I have been blessed with in life. I learned how to take responsibility for my actions without the need to blame myself. I learned that loving others starts with loving myself; and that I could not give to others what I did not have inside me. I learned that our worth cannot be measured by our titles, our accomplishments and our financial status. I learned to recognize and stop my negative self-talk gently, but consistently. I learned how to be humble by watching those in positions of power who remained modest. I learned how to be peaceful in the midst of chaos by watching those who remained centered through the most difficult times in their lives. I learned how to be accepting of people who were different from me by watching those who accepted me for who I was. I learned that to overcome challenges and achieve all that I desired, I had to change my focus from what was missing in my life, to all that I have been blessed with – from lack to abundance – from illness to health – from judgment to forgiveness - and from fear to love! I learned that feeling guilty won't change what we have done in the past; but guilt keeps us from working on ourselves in the present. After all, change takes effort and dedication; but to stay in the past and complain about our miseries requires no effort at all! Indeed, isn't this the reason so many of us don't take steps to discover what is getting in our way of experiencing true happiness?!

I believe, as human beings, each one of us comes into this world to fulfill a unique purpose. I now believe that everything that happened to me had to happen, to get me to where I am today:

- To learn to love unconditionally - I became a mother.
- To learn to forgive the unforgivable - I was sent to prison to forgive those who violently took me away from my family.
- To learn about inner strength and resilience – I had to deal with harsh realities of life at the age of 13…the tragic events in my country, my family and all that happened to me personally thereafter.

It took me decades finally to realize that my life long dream was never lost! It only manifested in a different form. It unfolded before me only when I was ready for it! The universe has given me the second chance to live my dream and I am not about to get in my own way this time.

Today I have a private coaching practice, and hold a full time job in a major public company. I have been fortunate enough to be part of community-based volunteer organizations such as Hospice Canada and Cummer Lodge long-term care home. It is extremely rewarding to be part of people's journeys and to support them along their paths. Working with people as a life coach is extremely rewarding for me. I get to listen to people to help them feel truly heard and understood. I get to acknowledge, validate and rephrase people's concerns to make sure I truly understand what they are going through. Sometimes it is what people don't say that interests me the most. I listen to thoughts and perspectives that limit people in some ways, hoping to encourage them to examine, what I call self-made blocks, more carefully. My sincere efforts, first and foremost, are to encourage people to treat themselves with the utmost love, compassion and respect. At times, I share some of the blocks that kept me from experiencing true happiness, to help people realize the similarities of our stories about life. My belief is that with the right support, people can move through their difficulties with less fear and pain. Sometimes I wonder if the entire trauma in my life affected me so severely because I did not have the right support to help me through it. Or perhaps, I was so convinced that no one could help, that even if the right support did show up, I did not recognize it.

My life has undoubtedly changed for the better. I am surrounded by much love and the support of my wonderful children, family and amazing friends. Within 8 years of my stay in Canada, two of my sisters joined us, including the baby sister I had to leave behind. One of my sisters lives in Europe and twice we have all been reunited as my father came to see us after more than a decade apart. As I greeted him at the airport, I saw an old man. Many of my past hurts and painful memories began to fade and I could make room for feelings of love and forgiveness. While I still struggle from time to time with my guilt about leaving my baby sister behind, especially during unhappy moments in her life, she and I have worked our way back together. Our closeness brings me great joy.

When I reflect back on my life and recognize how much time I have spent living in the past and worrying about the future, I feel overwhelmed. I do my best to stay present and enjoy and appreciate small pleasures in life today. Perhaps this is the best advice I can offer anyone.

EPILOGUE

A journey without a map is how I would describe my experience in writing this book. The unconditional support of my wonderful friends gave me strength; and Louise and Michael's priceless editorial feedback and suggestions kept me in line and focused. Yet, I still felt lost more often than not. I doubted myself every step of the way, thinking that I must be out of my mind to even dream of writing a book. Perhaps this was part of the process of transitioning "Kathy" the victim, to "Kathy" the strong, independent woman who is now more than adequate and a loving mother, a caring friend and an enthusiastic coach.

I must admit that I encountered many obstacles starting and finishing this project. First and foremost, I had to work through much anger, resentment, sadness and guilt that resurfaced while rehashing my past. As I wrote each chapter, I got to remember the most horrific experiences of my life I tried to bury inside me for almost three decades.

I had to translate my thoughts, feelings and experiences, most of which took place in Iran, from Farsi to English. This did not sound too difficult to me at first since I felt I had a good command of English, and writing was how I expressed myself best. Yet this project proved itself to be extremely difficult. I knew that I had to assume my target audience, North America, did not know much about what was happening in Iran at that time. I needed to provide them with enough background information to ensure I painted a clear picture. I wanted to be careful not to give out false impressions. Well, that was harder than I thought! It was a slow and painful process, but when I look back at all that I overcame to see this project through, I feel content that I have done my best to bring the message home.

Knowing that I still carried much pain and sadness inside me slowed me down thinking, that if I am not fully healed, I should not be writing this book. Such erroneous thoughts were draining me from the inside out. Until one day I had an epiphany! I came to realize and accept that my pain and sadness would be a small part of me for the rest of my life; yet, this did not mean that I would allow them to get in the way of moving forward and enjoying life to the fullest. I came to realize that I did not have to be perfect to be happy!

Though it took two years of hard work, sleepless nights and nightmares of Evin, and tearful days, in the end, it was well worth it. I am finally free!

In closing, I would like to confirm that while this was a true story of my life, some changes were made to protect the identity of those I spoke of in my book. Some locations, people's names and dates have been altered for safety reasons.

I believe a parable narrated by Eckhart Tolle in his book (The Power of NOW) best describes coaching.

A beggar had been sitting by the side of a road for over 30 years. One day a stranger walked by; "Spare some change"; mumbled the beggar, mechanically holding out his old baseball cab. "I have nothing to give you." Said the stranger. Then he asked, "What is that you are sitting on?" "Nothing." Replied the beggar. "Just an old box; I have been sitting on it for as long I can remember." "Ever looked inside?" Asked the stranger. "No."; Said the beggar. "What is the point; there is nothing in there." "Have a look inside." insisted the stranger. The beggar managed to pry open the lid; with astonishment, disbelief and illation he saw that the box was filled with gold.

I learned that men with machine guns are only the messengers of death… true executioners, the judge and the jury, are the well mannered men and women dressed in designers' suits, carrying leather cases and blackberries… Kathy A. Taheri